Cow Fart
Apocalypse

How a Zero-Carbon Emissions US Faced a Cow Flatulence Catastrophe...
A Political Parody-Thriller

E.M. Cooter

ISBN: 978-1-7372107-0-2 (Paperback)
ISBN: 978-1-7372107-1-9 (eBook)
V 1:03 07/13/2021

Cow Fart Apocalypse is an original work of fiction. The characters and dialogs in this parody are too farfetched to be believed... Or are they?

Any similarities to real-life people are the products of this author's vivid imagination, unless they're not. If the author has said something to upset someone, she/he/it (for the benefit of those who don't know their gender identity) is not sorry. Learn to laugh a little! This is a parody.

.

Prologue

AOC flashed a vacant grin at her American audience.

"As your President, The Most Honorable, Alexa Obtuse-Chavez, or AOC for short, or I prefer, Missy President... Like, I wanted to thank you for your vote, once more. The final Domination Voting Schemes tally from all 57 states is in and I received over 101% of your vote. More remarkably almost 105% of you Americans have voted. Wow, that's amazing. Special thanks to all of you, life-challenged people, who had passed away but still voted for me. As my way of saying thanks to everyone and because I don't want any of you to worry about the reports you may have read on that illegal news channel... You know, about the US being bankrupt... It just isn't true.

"Like, The Party just passed and I signed another Continuing Resolution this week, authorizing our treasury to print fifty-trillion more Party Dollars to cover everything. Plus, I'm happy to announce that I'm personally giving every registered Party member, a one hundred-thousand dollar raise, effective yesterday... Like, you're welcome."

AOC's portable screen went blank when it always told her exactly what to say next.

"I think that's it..."

She turned to the group of pasty-faced bankers, social media tycoons, attorneys and one ambassador at the other end of the office, all in fast discussion. "Ahh, I don't see any more words... Should I say anything else?"

She was already tired of this day, her—she counted out on her fingers—eighth day as president, now wanting it to end so she could play with the rest of the members of her Squadron. The song, *Whistle While You Work*, from the old Snow White cartoon popped into her head. She mouthed a whistle but didn't dare make a sound on camera, though she knew they would edit it out if she did.

The Chinese Ambassador, who just went by G, stopped his own monologue to address AOC. "You doing fine. Just sign off now." Then he returned his attention to his group, "Sorry for interruption..."

AOC returned an empty stare at the camera, which was hidden in the mobile screen they had placed in front of her desk. Just like the Picture Screens on each office wall, she knew a camera was there and live because of its green light. But her screen still didn't tell her what to say next.

"Well I think that's all. Like, this has been fun. Thanks... Oh and Gaia Earth bless me!" She smiled and stuck a thumb up in the air.

The light went from green to red.

An ancient military man with a chest full of medals burst into the Oval Office. "Missy President, we need you in the Situation Room ASAP!"

AOC gave her usual vacant smile, a deer-in-the-headlights gaze, at the general and then at the group who usually told her what to do next.

An elderly woman wearing a polyester pantsuit, standing nearby, leaned in and whispered in her ear, "ASAP means As Soon As Possible."

"Oh yeah. Thanks, HRC... HRC? Hey, did I make up that acronym or did someone else?"

HRC brayed her usual bellicose laugh; the one she used every time AOC asked questions like this. HRC said nothing more, but her cackling grew louder and louder.

AOC didn't get the joke.

The banker/lawyer/ambassador group stopped their conversations mid-sentence and glared at HRC, each of them showing their displeasure at her continued disruption.

AOC, not knowing what to do, giggled lightly, attempting to act like she understood why HRC was still laughing. Much of what she and the others did was a mystery to her.

"Missy President, we need you now," continued the general. With so many medals he looked like he permanently leaned forward and needed to prop himself up against the MLK bust by the doorway to keep himself from falling over.

"Missy President, you probably should follow him to the SITROOM," HRC said, still chortling a little.

"Okay, thanks Hil, I mean HRC," AOC said as she rose from her chair. She walked out of the Oval Office trailing the general, while the others followed behind her.

AOC exaggerated the general's scowl, tightening her facial muscles, drooping her shoulders and arms, all in her best effort to mimic the old general, who slowly lumbered in front of her.

She started to sing *Whistle While You Work*.

From The Horse's Mouth

"We set a goal to get to net-zero, rather than zero
emissions, in 10 years
because we aren't sure that we'll be able to fully get
rid of **farting cows** and airplanes that fast..."
~~~ Green New Deal FAQ Page
By Alexandria Ocasio-Cortez

"Maybe we shouldn't be eating a hamburger for
breakfast, lunch, and dinner.
Like, let's keep it real."
~~~ U.S. Rep. Alexandria Ocasio-Cortez, D-N.Y.

DAY ONE

Chapter 1
Seeing Green

Johnny Tipton sipped his very last Double Ristretto Venti Soy Nonfat Decaf Organic Iced Faux-Vanilla latte. He just didn't know it.

With his other hand, he attempted to hold back his newly coiffed pompadour from coming undone due to the frantic gusts of wind blowing in from the valley below. He huffed out a sigh in reply. He hated these self-serve power stations out in the country. Hell, he hated everything about rural areas. The whole rusticness of it all... Except for Moo Stations.

He could almost taste the dry soy burger and the side of krusty fries. It was his one reward to the whole deplorable trip. Many Party members, who had jobs that took them out into the country, often went to Moo Stations. Plus most other restaurant chains had gone bankrupt. So it was a common Party meeting place.

Still, it was puzzling why they didn't bring their savory plant-based franchises into urban centers. He didn't know much else about them other than they had become popular sometime after cows had been outlawed years ago.

Johnny's attention was drawn to a dull hum in the distance. A glistening movement in the sky that he instantly recognized as a Community Patrol drone. It was a reminder that even out here, in the middle of nowhere, The Party was always watching.

"JT? Are you almost done, dear," Muffy hollered from the passenger seat of their new Green Utopia, or what she called his GU.

That was another thing he hated; everyone used acronyms, including his sis-gendered partner, Muffy.

"Almost MT," he huffed.

As if on cue, the charging unit *pinged* a cheery tone, indicating his vehicle was fully charged.

He held up his wrist, the RFID chip inside instantly connecting with the station's computers, charging his bank account $4,952.28 for the fill-up.

This was an obscene amount to be charged for an EV fill-up. Yes, it was in the country. But it was part of his job to drive in the sticks. Not like he had any other choice for fill up. It should be free like everything else the government gave them, especially for bigwigs like him working for The Party.

As long as he was going to the Moo Station, he would get two orders of krusty fries and put them both on his expense account, just because his having to pay for the fill up really pissed him off.

Not that he would ever use "pissed off" out loud where Muffy could hear it. Muffy believed in the Party-speak and that words like, "pissed off" were another example of *hate-speech*. She would prefer his using less *ogre-esk*-like wording such as, *"he was full of emotion."*

JT pulled the charging handle out of his GU's receptacle and slammed it back in the station's single cradle. He scowled at the wind turbine mast, just a few meters away, which produced the power for his charge. Another reason why it should have been free.

His gaze was yanked further upward and away from the turbine to something foreign. And it wasn't a drone this time. Though he thought he'd heard a similar buzzing sound.

He wasn't sure what it was. Only that it did not belong in this green scape that so many (except him) found beautiful.

Among the blue skies were billowing patches of brown. Like clouds, only much lower and dirtier.

And they were moving fast… *Toward them.*

JT fixed his eyes—now dinner-plate-sized—on the muddy clouds due west of them, in the direction his car was pointed. He was both amazed and shocked by the swiftness of the little brown clouds, as he watched them congeal into a giant coffee-colored blob in the sky.

The mass picked up such speed that only then did he realize it would be upon them before he could hoof it around the back of the car and into the driver's seat, much less reverse them away from it.

Still, he didn't move.

His $300 latte slipped out of his hand, its eco-friendly cup cracking open like a ripe synthetic grapefruit on the ground, spilling its contents everywhere. The splat of wetness against his bare calves finally dislodged him from his moorings, though in the wrong direction.

He shuffled backward, while his whole body now shivered under the warm mid-day sun.

The low-lying gloom appeared to be coming from a vast field, in the valley below them. But he had not even bothered to look that way earlier. He had been more concerned with getting out of this hell hole and back to the city. And now he wished he had.

He continued to shuffle backwards, moving more rapidly. But it wasn't fast enough.

One of those ochre-colored clouds slid in from the other side and was directly above him.

Even before it consumed JT, he got a whiff of it.

In his panic, JT caught one of his high heels in the grassy road's rut and fell hard.

Dizzy from the smell and impact with the ground, he lifted his head and gazed at his Muffy. Her eyes were filled with tears—no doubt caused by the foul stench—her hands clutched at her throat, her tongue protruding out of her mouth. *It was too late for her as well.*

Flashbacks filled his head: when they first met at the BLM and ANTIFA rally in Portland; when they had gotten stoned; when they had protected sex and talked all night in their makeshift tent in the occupied zone. It was perfect then, other than the sewer smell and the lack of their showering for weeks.

This smell seemed even worse. He tried to recall this horrid stink, as it held some vague familiarity. And then he remembered...

Back when he was a kid and his fascist parents made him participate in 4H. He could not, at this moment, recall what that stood for, only that a bunch of right-winged nut jobs imprisoned animals for their own amusement, with the ultimate goal of— the taste of bile filled his mouth... eating them. The thoughts of it even now turned his stomach. But more so, he remembered that smell. That foul malodorous aroma, the root cause of which was supposed to have been outlawed, but somehow still existed... Cow farts.

This was his last thought, before the person known as Johnny Tipton, loyal member of The Party, was snuffed out of existence.

Chapter 2

Cow fart emergency

"Cow farts?" AOC asked, thinking she misunderstood her Chairman of Joint Chiefs of *something or another in the military*. She stared blankly at the giant Situation Room screen on the opposite wall, behind the stooped over general.

"Yes, ma'am," he turned and pointed at the largest image on the screen: a brownish blur moving in the sky. "It's a vast cloud of toxic cow farts and it's coming our way!"

AOC glared at the general not because of his apocalyptic proclamations but because of his use of "ma'am" when addressing her. She hated all sexist language by white men, and "ma'am" was among the worst. Then the horror of what the white-privileged, sexist-general had said hit her. "But wait, I thought we outlawed cows, like how is this even possible?"

"Yes we did ma'am. But this was confirmed by our head of the Office of Approved Science or OAS, to be, in fact, a giant cloud composed of cow farts."

Someone had to have caused this, she thought. Cows didn't just come back from the dead after they had been outlawed as part of the New Green New Deal law she had pushed through as a congresswoman, with Hil's help. Just before airplanes, all cows—the actual law listed some scientific name for cows which escaped her at that moment—were to be destroyed within five years. That was some time ago.

Maybe this was just the opportunity she was looking for.

So someone brought back cows that made these cow farts and now, as President, I have the means to exact punishment on the perpetrators, she thought.

She turned her head toward the military man who always shadowed her and was handcuffed to a briefcase—which did *not* in any way look like a football.

"General, isn't it time we play with the nuclear football... you know to punish the offenders?" She couldn't restrain the smile hiking up on her face, nor did she want to.

"Ma'am, that is not a toy."

"Duh!" AOC cocked back her head, exaggerating her drawn face. "It's not like I'm still a bartender. Though if I were, I'd have my bouncers here"—she pointed at her studly-looking Secret Service men—"throw you out, especially for referring to me as 'ma'am'. It's degrading. You hear me General?"

"Yes, ma—I mean, Missy President. My point is that we need to first discuss plans for evacuation, before we can discover who did this and then enact our retaliation plans."

She was still beaming at the visceral words she had so adeptly shot off at the general. They were almost as good as some of the Twats her handlers send out to her billion-plus followers on Twatter. She considered what the general had said before answering.

"Okay General, we'll wait on nuking the bastards—I always wanted to say 'let's nuke the bastards!'" She smiled at this, too. And then the smile lost all footing. "But what I don't understand is why we need to evacuate. It's not like cow farts are really deadly. Like, they're smelly, but that's it… Right?"

HRC stood up and physically nudged aside the general with an elbow, while sporting a toothy grin. "Well, Missy President." She clicked a little device at the big screen and a multi-colored bar graph appeared behind her, with lots of text.

This should be good, AOC thought, as she popped a handful of soy M&Ms into her mouth and chewed wildly... *Like a cow*, she bemused.

"You see, our internal surveys conducted around several Fakebook stories we've already posted this morning, show 97% of our followers are worried that such a cloud could be deadly."

"Ah, Fakebook." AOC mumbled and swallowed her mouthful. "Did you see my post this morning? I don't know who wrote it for me, but it was good. Personally, I thi—"

"Ma'am," the general interrupted, "can we get back to the situation at hand?"

That was it.

Just like one of those heated Old Joe speeches. When he was interrupted by a rude reporter, Joe unloaded a fiery fusillade of loosely strung together words which made no sense in a sentence but were wonderfully angry sounding. AOC responded with an equal measure of acrimony. "Secret Service People, I command you to shoot this man and drag his dead body away from me!"

This was something else she wanted to do when she became president, besides nuking a city - have one of her Secret Service people shoot someone on her command. She was curious if it looked the same as in a Tarantino film. She sat up in her chair in eager anticipation.

"Ah, Missy President... We don't do that... Well, maybe not in public view, you know, witnesses and all." HRC cackled.

While the two women bantered, the general spun on his heels and bolted for the door. But two members of AOC's detail were already there to collect him and escort him out of the Situation Room. Though they did so, disappointingly, without even drawing their weapons.

Even though no bullets were used, AOC found the whole exercise quite enjoyable.

AOC clapped her hands and dumped another handful of soy-candies into her mouth, "*Con-hinew, Hew*," AOC mumbled through swollen cheeks.

"Thanks, Missy President. So, The Party's survey-takers believe that this cloud, which appears to be headed our way in a matter of hours, might actually be deadly. We've had reports of people collapsing and appearing to have died after being exposed to it.

Our psychologist teams from OAS, believe

this is because the population has not been exposed to cow flatulence for years. And many never have."

AOC swallowed. "But is it really, you know... deadly?"

"It doesn't matter. People think it is. So that's the story. Besides, remember our motto: Never let a crisis go to waste. And *this* crisis will provide the perfect excuse we need to get the main Party leaders in DC away from their homes so that we can upgrade their Picture Screens with our TLS, which is our Telescreen Listening Software.

"Remind me again, what's *our Telescreen Listening Software?*"

"Oh, it's a Party joke. It's the Picture Screens, but we call them Telescreens, after George Orwell's 1984", which is sort of The Party bible..." HRC noticed that AOC wasn't understanding her. "It's what we were talking about earlier. Using this, we can see and hear who is planning seditious... I mean, see who is talking about overthrowing The Party and your administration."

"Oh right, I remember now." AOC nodded and then lifted the entire bowl of the remaining soy candies and emptied them into her awaiting trap. Her mouth was so full she thought she might have to spit some back, but that would have been kind of disgusting. So, she chomped away.

"Missy President?" HRC called to her from across the room.

Oh yeah, I was about to have to make a decision.

She chewed wildly and then swallowed the wad full, choking as she was trying to get them all down.

"Yeah... Hil. *Peas* continue."

"As I was saying, this plan will work. All we need is your signature on this Emergency Powers Declaration."

On cue, her cabinet member, AS, who preferred the pronouns "they," "them," and "their"—though some of her cabinet called *them* "Ass" behind *their* back—slipped a tablet in front of her with a stylus. At the bottom was a place for her to sign. She didn't remember hearing what the plan was and only now hearing it as an Emergency Powers Declaration. A thought bubbled up from her memory, long before she got the role to play a congresswoman: One time, when the Majority Leader, NP told Congress to sign a giant bill and that *they could read it after they signed it*... That was back when they used to print their laws on paper, which required them to kill trees—*which never harmed us*—all to make that paper.

AOC touched the bottom of the tablet and it said page 15,252 out of 15,252 pages. *Wow, that would have been a lot of paper! No way am I going to read that.*

Well, if it was good enough for NP—rest her soul— it's good enough for me.

She scratched her "A O C" autograph, in big block letters, on the bottom of the tablet in digital ink.

Looking up, she handed it back to AS. If she remembered right, *they* were using Adelina Shift as *their* actual name now. She shivered when she caught a glance of *their* eyes, which looked bigger and shiftier than ever. Though, AS looked a lot better today, in *their* nice, printed dress and pink nylons, than *they* did when *they* went by Adam.

AS snatched the tablet back, tapped on it a few times and gave a thumbs up to HRC, who turned to the Picture Screen on the western wall. The picture transformed from a still image of President BHO into something similar to a mirror. She whispered to it and announced with a smile, "It is done, Missy President. Now, let's get you to back to the Oval so you can read your announcement."

Chapter 3
Don't believe your lying eyes

"Chris Bozo here from CCPN Washington. I am standing here, staring directly into the rear end of an oncoming toxic fart-cloud of death, stampeding its way directly at me. I do this without any fear and..."

A pedestrian, not used to seeing someone in a clear hazmat suit, much less an older muscle-punk wearing only a Speedo underneath, stopped in front of the camera to gawk at the sight before him.

"Get the hell out of my shot or I will kick your ass," Bozo yelled. He took a step forward threateningly, with a fist pumped into the air.

The pedestrian yawned and then thought better of further engaging this crazy-looking person. Bozo smiled wide at the man's exit and then realized what he'd just done, in front of the camera.

Speaking through his teeth he huffed, "Wait, you didn't get that on camera, did you?"

"Chris, can you hear me?" Don Lemming pseudo-begged the screen that showed their nearly naked correspondent in his bubble suit, pretending he didn't hear anything that had just happened. Lemming pivoted in his chair to his right, facing the studio's main camera. "I'm afraid we lost Chris, who is out there in left—I mean the field, risking his very life, to cover this late-breaking story for us all. May Gaia Earth be with you, my friend."

A bold graphic materialized over Lemming's image on one of the two large television screens, separated by a main camera. It was there so Lemming could see what his viewers saw. The graphic wasn't obvious at first, as letters spun around and around. But the letters materialized into words and then the words formed, "Cow Fart Apocalypse!" Lightning bolts exploded out of the now pulsating graphic, as brown clouds billowed from behind, while sounds of cows mooing in accompaniment to a dramatic musical score played in the background.

It was the first time he'd heard the soundtrack. It was just conjured up by the CCPN creative types in Beijing. It trailed off and was followed by the normal CCPN theme music. A familiar voice—heard only by him through his earpiece—told Lemming to do his intro.

He read his screen, word for word.

"This is Don Lemming from CCPN Central, reporting on the newest crisis which some experts say may kill millions. We were just cut off from Chris

Bozo, in the field. We'll bring Chris back when we reacquire his signal"—Lemming couldn't help but smile at this one, sure that the CCPN producers on the ground were giving Bozo the same new script he'd just been given, and telling him to stick to it this time.

Lemming turned to his right to another camera and set of TV screens on that wall. He spoke the teleprompter's words. "I'm here with Chung Zin Lu, an expert with ten PhD's from Hainan University, to discuss bovine flatulence. He is here to give us a heaping shovelful of facts on why farts, from what were believed to be extinct cows, have just appeared out of nowhere. Dr. Lu, please explain."

Lemming blinked at the screens in front of him, waiting for his queue to continue his dialog. The green room in which Lemming sat was shown to be a giant shining glass studio in New York City. That was the image their millions of viewers saw. It was actually a small room in Lemming's Los Angeles home.

He suspected that the real-life demure, black-haired man he was interviewing was almost seven-thousand-miles away to the east. The man's talking image appeared on a screen to the right of his teleprompter screen, separated by a camera. Lemming knew that the geniuses in the back rooms of The Party's main station in Beijing would make it look as if Dr. Lu was in the made-up NYC studio with him, seemingly only a couple of feet away.

Like all Party members, they both had to just play their parts.

"Well," Dr. Lu said in a stereotypically thick Chinese accent, "Cow flatulence is not something Americans have seen in many years, after they were declared illegal by The Party. So this is something new. It appears that—"

"Sorry to interrupt Dr. Lu, but I think our viewers are most interested in whether the toxic cloud of death will reach them?" Lemming cut in, reading the words that rolled down his teleprompter screen. "As you heard in Missy President's broadcast just minutes ago, an evacuation is about to be declared on a large section of the DC area. Could this expand to other areas, depending on where the winds blow?"

"Well," the Doctor continued, "It is quite possible that the cloud may reach other areas. And yes, it is very deadly. It could kill—"

Lemming couldn't help himself. He went off script. "I'm sorry to interrupt you again, Dr Lu." Lemming stuck a finger in the air. "We are talking about cow farts here, right? I mean, no one actually died from inhaling them before The Party outlawed cows, did th—"

Lemming saw a red-light flash rapidly on his teleprompter screen and his earpiece crackled with one word, in an unmistakably familiar voice: "Stop!"

He had pushed it too far. This came directly from CCPN Central, telling him to stop this line of questioning immediately. His action was akin to questioning The Party's mantra about cow farts, no matter how stupid the whole thing sounded. He knew better and shuttered a little when he thought about being sent to one of those VETC reeducation facilities as punishment. Only last week, Rachel Madness went off the air after questioning AOC's intelligence on her broadcast. She hadn't been heard from since.

He would stop.

Lemming turned to the middle screen to face a new flashing green light above a different camera. The screen above it stated "Alert." This was a new alert handed down directly from The Party to approved news outlets, like CCPN.

When the words appeared on the screen, he dutifully read them. "This is an alert. Everyone in the following areas of DC are ordered to evacuate: Massachusetts Avenue Heights, Kamalorama, Obama Park, Pelosi Gardens, and GeorgeFloydtown. Private coaches are headed to you, for your immediate transport to safe areas. You have thirty minutes to finish your meals and exit your residences. Leave all belongings behind, including your tablets. Everyone else in the DC and outlying areas are ordered to remain in your homes until you receive further orders."

The light turned from green to solid red.

Lemming turned to his far left to face a new screen flashing an alert. This one came from a different area of their Beijing office news desk, giving them the so called "local news". He suspected most of this was made up, but he was paid nine figures to read the news and smile on camera, not to report. He didn't really care what it said.

"And this just in... A terrorist was just arrested in Virginia. We now turn to Ashley Jiang in the field to give us the terrifying details."

The screen to the right of the two, blinked an image of Ashley wearing her usual mini-skirt, pencil-thin heals, and a ridiculously low-cut blouse, meant to show off every curve of her absurdly enhanced feminine figure. She held a microphone to her overly rouged lips, now pursed and ready for her delivery. She was standing in front of a farmhouse in a rural part of Virginia, with yellow tape separating her from the house.

"Thank you, Don. Just moments ago, an unidentified man, holding out in this rural compound, was found to have had a stash of illegal weapons and food. This video footage was shot mere moments ago as federal authorities arrested the terrorist suspect."

Lemming and Jiang waited for their audience to see the pre-recorded tape of the arrest by the armed officials of the Firearms and Insurrectionists Authority or FIA, each in full body armor. A handcuffed man with a canvas hood over his head, was led out of the farmhouse to an awaiting armored truck. Another official followed, holding out for the cameras with what looked like a BB gun and one small box, before he stepped into the truck. A third official hoisted up two cases of plastic-wrapped food into the truck, stepped inside and slammed the doors behind him.

They sped away from the camera, which followed it for a moment and then abruptly returned to Ashley. She was looking down, adjusting her blouse, when her head snapped up to face the camera. Her face changed from disgust to fake smile. "The forty-year-old man had a 22-caliber, military-designed, machine-gun, assault rifle, with what was described as a mega-death, rocket launcher. The domestic terrorist also had in his possession 20 rounds of what I am told is long-rifle ammunition. Yes, you heard me right, not short-rifle, but long-rifle. My experts tell me it's enough to start a war."

"Oh—my—god, Ashley." Lemming jumped in, just when his teleprompter told him to. "I am shaking my head with amazement that a civilian could get his hands on such machines of war, so many years after the Second Amendment was overturned in that landmark 30 to 6 decision."

"Yes, Don. But *that* was not the worst offense... This white-supremacist, racist, right-wing-fascist, domestic terrorist had also committed the federal offense of hoarding. My experts tell me he had over *two weeks* of food in his possession."

They both feigned abject astonishment.

Lemming's thoughts drifted to where the arrested man and the truck were probably headed. He had no doubt. The man was headed straight to one of the VETC facilities in the area.

He shivered at this thought, but then quickly manufactured a smile for the middle camera.

He turned and read the words of the new alert just displayed.

Chapter 4

Where the cows now roam

The bright red banner on the TV screen read, "This unauthorized broadcast has been shut down by ReAD for violating Party guidelines."

Colin Backwater sighed. He punched the channel button on the controller, moving from the breakroom's preferred channel and its now foreboding message, to The Party TV's CCPN, just as his boss walked in.

"Are you seeing this, boss?" Colin asked, pointing at the empty breakroom's TV. A graphic pulsated lightning bolts on the bottom, while a split screen of various idiots argued about the most recent manufactured crisis.

His uncle, Noel Franklin, the owner of Abound Green Industries, walked up to the giant coffee machine and placed his green Abound cup in the receptacle and commanded, "Party Black, full cup."

Colin asked again, thinking that Noel hadn't heard him. "They shut down the Patriot channel again. I had to go to CCPN. Can you believe what's happening?"

Noel paused before taking a sip from his steaming coffee to examine the TV. The elderly black man wore a crown of perfectly groomed silvery hair and his overalls were as crisp as the rest of his persona. He spoke from behind his cup. "Yep, been on all morning. Some snowflakes died of stress after getting a whiff of a cow fart and now Missy Snowflake has declared an emergency, or some such bullshit." He took in a giant gulp from his cup, in spite of it being piping hot. Colin never understood the whole coffee-drinking thing anyway.

"It's not..." Colin glanced at his feet and then back up to Noel, "you know, from our cows, is it?"

He watched his uncle's emotionless face change instantly. It twisted and turned, until the man lunged forward and spat out a mouth-full of coffee. He first laughed like he'd heard the funniest joke ever. Then hacked like a cancer patient in hospice, after smoking a whole pack of illegal cigarettes.

Colin studied his uncle, trying to understand if the coffee just went down the wrong pipe or if he had a problem with what he'd asked.

It was a full minute before he spoke. "Good God, man," his voice coming out more gravelly than usual. He coughed some more. "Don't do that shit when I'm drinking coffee."

"I know. It was a stupid question," Colin added, doing his best to show some embarrassment.

"Come with me," Noel motioned for Colin to follow him. He coughed again while adding more coffee to his cup, and headed out the door.

Colin watched his uncle scamper through the first doorway, like a younger man. Then the second door, its pressurization generating a muffled *whoosh*-sound.

After Noel was through both doors, Colin followed. The loud *whoosh* of the second door ushered in the full aroma of Noel's precious Angus cows. A cacophony of moos and clattering noises from below enveloped him and yet he felt at home once more, just as he knew his uncle did.

Noel parked himself against the end of the center walkway, built to give whoever occupied it a bird's eye view of the whole operation, twenty-five feet below. With his coffee cup set upon the railing, he waited on his dias-like platform for Colin to catch up, no doubt so he could deliver one of his preachy "teaching moments".

Colin did not mind. There was no one he respected more. Every time he saw the giant indoor farm Noel had secretly created, it made his uncle look even more saintly. Considering he ran this underground operation (under the threat of arrest) and could potentially get his brain reset by The Party if he were caught. It always brought Colin to a sense of awe when he looked at what his uncle had accomplished.

Stopping before Noel, Colin gave the facility another glance. It was the size of a football field, packed with an offering more illegal than an Evangelical church service: Cows. Over a thousand of them.

"You see this," Noel spread out his arms like a prideful Moses before the Red Sea. He was referring to the whole operation: the farm, the cows, the processing, the structures, and that everything was nearly one-hundred-percent automated so that just a few employees were needed to tend to them. Those few were family or long-time family friends, as well as members of the Patriots. That meant less chance of Party spies.

"As you know, everything here is cut off from the outside world. The atmosphere is completely pressurized, so there is no way any of the gasses inside can get out. It's one way we can quietly produce steaks and hamburger meat for all of the red-blooded Americans who still exist in this screwed up country of ours, all while pretending to be a 'green energy'"—he made air-quotes with his fingers—"company for all of the idiot Leftists who back the public side of our operations. So, even if it was possible for a bunch of cow farts to turn into a billowing stink-cloud that kills, it didn't come from us."

"Yeah, I just thought... I don't know what I thought."

Colin was sure that the Patriots were somehow involved, and he knew that Noel was a high-level member, whereas Colin was just a low-level grunt in the decentralized Patriot organization. When he joined, Colin was told that the Patriots learned one thing from the Freedom Fighters in Afghanistan and from Al-Qaeda in Iraq: decentralization allowed Patriot Units (like cells) to be flexible so they could operate independently. That way, if the unit's members were caught or broken up, there would be little to no way to connect them to any of the other units or the main leaders, who were unknown to almost all Patriots. Most members believed there was a high-level group, they referred to as the Brotherhood, who met and planned from time to time. Colin suspected Noel was part of that Brotherhood.

He didn't want to push his questioning too far. He didn't want Noel to break trust with him. But he was too curious to let it lie. Since his Unit Commander had just notified him to be ready for Operation CF. He wondered now if that stood for Operation Cow Fart. It seemed ridiculous. But in a way, it made sense. He had to press further, but carefully, with his uncle.

"Do you think the Patriots had something to do with this?"

"Does that question really pass the smell test?" Noel chortled.

"Ha-ha. But remember, after you hired me last summer, that mystery group who said they knew my parents? They had some scientific project that dealt with our manure. The talk was that they were associated with the Patriots. Some argued that it was a way to bring back beef, by making the Commies think about it. Others said it was something bigger."

"Sounds to me like you should spend more time focusing on your job, and not listening to all the tongue-waggers around here."

"Come on, Noel. I'm being serious here." Colin locked his hands on his hips and glared at him. He wanted his uncle to know he wasn't going to be dissuaded. He also knew this was what Noel appreciated about him: a dogmatic need to find the answer to a question.

"Perhaps you're right. Come on, son. Clock out and then meet me at Moo Burger. I'm buying." Noel hesitated as one of the oversized pockets of his overalls buzzed. It was obviously his tablet, but he didn't move to answer it. Noel's head tilted down and then back up at Colin, though not directly.

Then his uncle's whole demeanor changed. He pulled out a tablet from a different pocket than the one that had buzzed. As if he were making a show of it, he touched the screen and turned away from Colin. Then he said, "I maybe late, so don't rush over there." He put his tablet back in his pocket and waited. For what, Colin didn't know.

I guess I've been dismissed, Colin thought. "Thanks Noel. I would love that." Colin spun around intending to dash away, eager to get changed and go to Moo Burger. He hoped to learn more, if not from Noel, then from some of the other Patriots there. But he paused and peeked back at Noel, who had now pulled out a different tablet from the pocket that buzzed. With his back to Colin, Noel held it up, and with the red Flashgram app open, the letters were big enough to make out the first few words, "Phase 2: Operation Cow Fart."

Colin turned back to the exit and stepped away slowly, not looking to see if Noel noticed him. Mostly he didn't want the man to see his smile.

Once through the pressurized door, Colin beat a path to his locker, already unlatching his overalls. He quickly slipped out of them and put on his dress trousers, tie, and jacket. After a minute of prep and glancing at the mirror, he thought he looked every bit the part of a Party businessman who worked for one of the top green companies in the country.

Grabbing his keys and real calfskin covered laptop—he told everyone it was imitation—he headed out of the locker room and into the reception area.

"I'm out for the day, BC," he said, without looking at their pretty receptionist. He was too excited to banter.

"Okay, CB. See you tomorrow."

Once outside, he glanced up at the sky, not really expecting to see the brown cloud that was causing all the fuss. But something did catch his eye.

It was one of the many Community Patrol drones that buzzed around, looking for any disapproved behavior. This one zipped by overhead, going through its normal patrol of its nine square mile grid of this mostly rural area. The black and white drone had "Protect and Serve" stenciled on its underside. Before his father died, he was told that this was the motto of all police agencies. Then they were disbanded by the federal government and police officers were replaced by drones, overseen by one of an uncountable number of federal enforcement agencies, often including the FIA or ReAD.

Colin submissively looked down when he really wanted to shake a fist at the thing. He wasn't worried about doing something wrong, because he looked like a Party member. But the damned things were so obtrusive. He lived for the day when some of the freedoms his father told him about were returned to his country.

Perhaps that day had already started.

He climbed into his electric truck and pressed the starter. A monotoned voice asked, "Destination?" and Colin said, "Manual." The car responded, "Accepted". The steering wheel turned green to indicate it was active. Most people used their vehicle's automated controls but Colin preferred to drive himself.

He looked at his map screen to check on the traffic to Moo Station and was surprised to see a map of Beijing, China, and not rural Virginia. He remembered talk of the GPS and mapping programs going out of whack. Now he saw it firsthand.

His excitement grew.

Were the Patriots behind all this? Were they getting ready to finally mount their resistance to The Party, which had long since taken over and destroyed their country? Was this the day?

He punched his accelerator and swung out of Abound Green Industries' parking lot, trying to visualize what real freedom might look like.

Chapter 5
A useful tool

"Hey, that was my best broadcast. *Ever!*" AOC exclaimed, leaning back in her gaming chair at the Oval's Resolute Desk.

She glanced down at her recent handiwork. She had used the sharp tip of some newly discovered old pen called a quill to etch "I was here" into the wood of the desk drawer. She smiled at the thought that this desk was *like, a million years old, or something*. And now her thought and name were part of that history... Her smile slid off her face as she realized that no one would know who "I" was. She'd have to sneak back in when no one was looking and add her initials. She looked up at the Picture Screen— HRC called it a Telescreen—and wondered if someone was watching her right now.

"Missy President?"

She sat bolt upright, her head snapping toward the voice. "Yes, HRC. It wa-was good, no?" she asked.

"Oh, yes MP. The Party has already given you high marks. They especially loved the tears at the end."

AOC's smile regained ground, now stretching ear-to-ear. "I know, that part was really good, wasn't it? When the bartender thing wasn't working, I went into acting. I tried out for a part in some movie that involved crying, and got the part playing a congresswoman instead. Then... Well, you know all that. Anyway, I found I could muster tears pretty easily. It sure comes in handy when you're in the public eye."

The Oval's east entrance popped open unannounced. Several people she didn't recognize paraded inside with AS (preferred pronoun they/their/them) following behind. She thought of how many referred to the big-eyed cabinet member as "Ass" and she snickered again at this. AS had an armful of faux-leather folders. Trailing AS was *their* assistant holding a box of gold-plated pens, and on the caboose of this train from bizarroville was the WH photographer, who sported his own crazy getup of purple. "All aboard the signing train!" AOC huffed. "Choo-Choo!"

The rest of the rush of people, some of them she now recognized as being part of her Cabinet, took seats on the couches and chairs at the other end of the Oval Office, probably in preparation for the next boring meeting they had planned for her.

AS had already thrust open one of the faux-leather folders in front of her, while on her left *their* assistant handed AOC a pen. She had done this several times during her short time in the White House, and she understood this was a big part of the role she was playing. She grabbed the pen, scribbled her autograph—also something not of her own design, but something that she had to learn for her role. With a smile, she held up the folder so the signed portion was shown forward. The photographer snapped her picture. Then onto the next.

She didn't bother to ask what she was signing. The Party did all of the work in deciding what rules she made, the wording of the rules, and how to communicate the new rules to the proles—she was told that term was also out of *1984* to refer to the common folks—that The Party ruled over. As HRC explained it, The Party built an expensive car, hired the driver and mechanics to handle its maintenance, and even provided the electricity to charge the vehicle. AOC's role was solely to be the decorative hood ornament. And she was just fine with that, thank-you.

Just as her signing hand was starting to cramp up, she was done and HRC was hurriedly ushering her out of her seat toward the back western door. AOC turned to the group, already thick in conversation. She was about to ask what was happening, but before she could get a word out, she was pushed through the doorway.

HRC said it was time for her 11AM meeting with her Reality Czar, KH, with whom she had previously worked as a congresswoman. After this she was off to meet with her ReAD (Reality Against Disinformation) committee to burn some books.

KH was already waiting for her just outside the door, wearing her usual forced grin, like a Halloween mask that she never took off.

As they approached, KH immediately thanked HRC for the hand-off. HRC then left them to return to the Oval and the meeting AOC wasn't a part of.

Just as well. She hated the constant meetings and their monotony.

"Hello Missy P," KH said. "Thanks again for the appointment. This is so much better than the Vice President or even the President jobs that the Party had given me earlier. It's especially great because I've always believed that reality is what you make of it."

KH's head wrenched from side to side and then back, "Ah, or what The Party makes of it." As they began walking slowly together, KH's glare hung onto a Picture Screen they were approaching midway down the hallway, just a few feet away. AOC forgot just how flighty KH was.

"You're welcome, KH. I was told you were the only choice because you did what the Party wanted of yo—"

KH abruptly stopped them in a doorway. Again, her head swung wildly in one direction and then the other, as if she were concerned that someone besides AOC might hear what she was about to say. In a voice barely above a whisper, "Ah, sorry to interrupt you MP, but shouldn't we be getting out of DC now, you know with the cow fart cloud coming our way?"

AOC wondered this too, and now felt the same kind of nervousness she had felt earlier, when she first heard about this. The unanswered question still lingered in her mind: Could these cow farts really be deadly? HRC said it didn't matter and told her twice already not to worry. "The Party will take every precaution." But AOC saw the reports about how people exposed to the cloud immediately collapsed and some may have even died.

"Missy President, do you need assistance?" demanded, more than asked, one of her Secret Service people, who had silently appeared beside her.

"I'm okay," AOC responded with a turn of her head, as she looked back at KH. She thought of the words HRC told her. *Your role is to follow our direction. If you do that, we will keep you safe and give you a lavish lifestyle only enjoyed by the highest elites of The Party.*

AOC turned on her confident face. "You have nothing to worry about KH. The Party will take care of us. If the cloud gets too close, they will get us to someplace safe."

KH nodded, accepting what was told to her.

AOC couldn't help but feel good at having done something on her own.

"So where are we going?" AOC asked.

"We're here at the Situation Room for a special op by the ReAD. But before we enter, I wanted to give you an update on our fight against disinformation and domestic reality extremism.

AOC yawned.

"For one, although we closed the Patriot's TV broadcast down, they've already found other servers and they're back up again broadcasting."

"Do you know where?" AOC asked.

"It's Russia."

"Wait," thinking she heard wrong. "I thought that whole Russia-did-it-thing was all made up and they were on our side."

"Well yes, it was, and they are. Remember, we just honored Putin for his many decades as president. But we think it's some rogue group and not their government."

"Okay, now I'm confused. I thought Putin was dead."

"Well, they actually brought him back to life."

"I'll bet that was handy for their party."

"Yes, The Party's working on something similar for NP."

AOC gave KH a stern look. "Okay, now I know you're just kidding me."

They stood before the Situation Room's door, pondering the possibilities in silence.

KH gave a phony smile. "This leads me to the next update on the arrest and reeducation of Patriots."

"Are we going to go in?" AOC motioned to the door, now interested in the subject and the prospect of what was going to happen in the Situation Room.

"Yes, of course."

KH opened the door. A large group of military brass and several Chinese ambassadors were seated around the Situation Room's large table. They all jumped to their feet as AOC and KH entered.

"Be seated," KH stated to the group. "I was just about to fill in Missy President on our efforts to stop The Patriots."

There was a light chatter among a few of the military folks; a conclusion to an argument that must have started earlier. AOC found her seat at the head of the long table. KH walked around to the front, where an assistant handed her a laser pointer.

Damn, I want one, AOC thought. She'd have to ask HRC for one.

"As I was about to say, arrests of Patriots are up by 9000% this week. We expect a bust of one of the real-life cow burger places in a rural county of Virginia." KH glanced at the multiple clocks on the wall, each showing a different time in different countries around the world, maybe trying to find the one that applied to Virginia. AOC found all the time zones confusing. Besides, she did not need a clock when every minute of her day was scrutinized by The Party.

A general, this one tall and studly looking with a similar number of medals as the general she'd kicked out of the room, stood up straight as a board and grabbed the laser pointer from KH.

Guess he needed it more than KH did.

He looked directly at AOC. "We're about to go to a live feed of the raid."

KH cut in, "But we can only watch for ten minutes. Then we have the book burning ceremony to attend with the ReAD committee. She smiled, her *I'm-better-than-you-are- smile* and stepped back.

The big screen splashed multiple video feeds all at once.

"What you're seeing, Missy President is from a set of CP drones above a Moo Station restaurant."

Chapter 6
Do as I say, not as I do

"Those of you who are not in the evacuation areas, please remain indoors until the threat has passed," Don Lemming continued. "Further, the Center for Disease Enforcement or CDE has recommended that you find your old cloth masks and wear them once again."

Lemming thought back to the last time everyone wore cloth masks. The joke was if you could smell someone's fart with a mask on, how could it protect you against a virus? Masks certainly weren't going to get better with age, much less protect people from this toxic fart cloud... assuming it was anywhere near the threat level he was reporting.

His gaze wandered from his script to his own image displayed on the main screen, with the undulating Cow Fart Apocalypse graphic in the top right corner, and on the bottom, the constant scrolling chyrons. Often these updated his audience on "news" events occurring during the broadcast. One chyron stated with authority, "GPS System Destroyed by Patriot Terrorist Group." *Who knew how much of that was really true?*

But often they displayed quotes from his broadcast, which had supposedly come from his own mouth and that of his guests, even before they were actually spoken. It always made him wonder if anyone in his audience had a clue that his show was completely scripted. He knew better. The common proles, for whom the CCPN channel was designed, were so indoctrinated by The Party's language, they would never even consider the possibility that "news programs" like his were all made up. Yes, there were real-life, active stories going on, but they were all manipulated and controlled by The Party. Everyone bought it hook, line, and sinker.

It was truly like they were all drugged or had a disease that kept them from being able to question the narrative they were being fed. Instead, everyone just parroted the same regurgitated lies over and over. He often thought of Leftism as a disease. At one time, he suffered from it. But he was paid so well to spew their crap, none of it bothered him. He wasn't a Party loyalist as much as he was a money loyalist.

A booming Chinese voice barked curses through his earpiece.

Lemming was shocked to see that he had missed much of what he was supposed to read from his teleprompter screen. Its words kept rolling down the screen without him.

He'd have to ad lib.

"Ahhh, the nation's GPS system has been so screwed up by hackers that chaos has struck the country blah-blah-blah. It appears to have been done by none other than the infamous Patriots, which Missy President and the Party have once again deemed domestic terrorists. Here are some reports we're getting..." While he waited for a good place to read, he summed up some of their reports.

"Many Party members have found their cars turning off the road into buildings or into other cars, rather than onto their programmed routes, because the systems no longer could determine which direction was left or right. For example..."

He started reading the teleprompter again.

"One elite Party member claimed to have been directed to an illegal house church, instead of their home."

Lemming struggled to hold back a snicker.

"Ahhh, one Deseray Nocolor says that after being forced to eat a meal and sing Christian songs for an hour, the group gave him freshly baked cookies and directions home... one block away."

"In a more serious incident, a Party member, driving his family to a BLM rally, drove right into the oncoming fart cloud. CP drone video footage"—a grainy video flashed on the screen—"appears to show no movement in the car. The family may very well have perished."

"So, my friends, The Party advises everyone to remain indoors and not drive at this time."

When the camera's red light went on and his teleprompter screen told him to face the right screen now, he wasn't sure what to do because he was already facing that screen. So he turned to his other screen. Sure enough the left-most screen was green and his teleprompted words were already rolling—he was behind again.

"We now return you to our coverage of the *Cow Fart Apocalypse... when cows go bad.*" He couldn't help himself with that addition. He was feeling very rebellious lately. "We are joined by Bennington Arnold, the former manager of a California Moo Station and author of a new tell-all book, *The Great Cow Cover-up - How Moo Stations Secretly Sold Illegal Cow Burgers on The Side.* Bennington appears to have predicted this very crisis.

"Mr. Arnold, welcome to the program."

"Thank you, Don it's a pleasure to be with

you and talk about my book, which is currently available on my website at—"

"—Sir," Lemming cut in, "you have been quoted as saying, 'We will, one day, face a cow fart apocalypse that will be biblical.' How could you have known something like this might actually occur?"

"Yes, Don. As I was saying, in my book, currently available for sale on Big River for $299.99, I chronicle the Moo Station's illegal cow raising operation and how they—"

"—Thank you, Mr. Arnold. I'm sorry to interrupt, but we are now joined by our intrepid reporter on the ground, Chris Bozo, on the DC Mall. Chris?"

The video feed started, showing Bozo, still in his clear hazmat suit, wearing only a Speedo underneath. Lemming now remembered Bozo had used this suit on a Bubble Boy story some years ago. Bozo must not know the difference. The clear plastic suit was cloudy from his breathing and perspiration. He was performing dumbbell curls for two women in clear plastic skirts and shirts—the current dress fad for women—which showed off the frilly undergarments they wore underneath. Luckily for their cameras, these women had the figures and colorful undies so the audience would be distracted from Bozo's escapades.

CCPN cameras always found the necessary amount of T and A to add to their ratings. It was like the drugs that The Party pushed... One more form of control over the country's proles.

"Watch this, ladies. I'm very strong."

The women giggled through their old threadbare cloth masks. Lemming assumed that like these women, lots more people would start wearing these since the new CDE mandate. Ever since the CDC changed into the Center for Disease Enforcement, people have willingly followed their mandates.

Bozo still didn't realize he was live.

"Chris, are you hearing me? We're on the air." Lemming laid it on thick for his TV audience. Though he had no idea what would be in the final broadcast or blacked out, based on what CCP elites decided was fit for viewing. For all he knew, his broadcast would be scrubbed altogether for a rerun of *The White Terrorist Threat in America*, one of their more popular shows.

Bozo froze mid-curl and turned his head to the camera. He snuck the dumbbell behind his back, as if that would erase his performance from the TV audience's collective minds. "Hello Don. I'm still here, on the National Mall. Terror has struck the citizens of DC, leaving the city in utter chaos." Bozo leaned over to lower the dumbbell, and the two woman he was performing for waved at the camera.

"Those few who have ventured outside, have pulled out their old COVID-19 masks, in hopes of protecting themselves from the oncoming killer cow-fart-cloud." He motioned the two blondes to come forward, each of whom was now basking in their new-found limelight.

"I'm here with Misty and Frisky"—"Hi" the women yelled back in unison—"These two beauties are among the few still left on the street, waiting for Armageddon to hit DC."

Yeah, because they're too stupid to go home, Lemming thought.

"Back to you Don."

"Hey, you said you'd mention I'm an actress," hollered the taller of the two, before that image went black.

The main screen returned to Lemming in the studio, with the already tiring Cow Fart Apocalypse logo and music. Then the loud sound and graphic, "UPDATE!" reappeared.

"We're back at our New York studio for more details about the cow fart cloud, which is reported to be only fifty miles from Washington DC and picking up steam." *He was on a roll now.*

"The US Military has been dispatched around all major cities, to keep the peace, as spontaneous peaceful demonstrations have broken out." Video showed various scenes of fires and riots in multiple cities.

"Additionally, scientific teams from the OAS are on the ground, in and around the Capitol. Based on their recommendation, Dulles International Airport, which is in the fart-cloud flight path, has been closed.

"OAS teams will continue to report back to us so we can tell you when the threat is over."

Lemming turned to his right camera and continued. "In other news, the state of Wyoming has been returned to Native Americans.

"Earlier today, Missy President held a news conference where she made this stunning announcement."

A video started, from a local affiliate, showing AOC standing in front of the Wyoming State capitol building. Lemming knew it was actually a green screen effect and AOC had not been to Cheyenne, Wyoming today, or ever, much less be able to identify where it actually was.

"Because the white man has taken too much from the true *native* citizens of this country, The Party wishes to offer a small repayment for our past sins, by giving back the State of Wyoming."

The screen now showed Lemming back in the studio.

"Local tribal leaders," Lemming read, "said they thank Missy President for this gesture. They are now planning a new chain of casinos on what is currently State property, followed by a mass relocation of tribal members into the homes built for them by the white invaders." *That should be good for a 1% bump in the polls*, Lemming thought.

Lemming saw his main screen go green and so he turned to it.

"—This just in.

"We are getting reports of a shake up during this apocalypse, with a major ReAD operation coming up at a Moo Station restaurant. We have live footage of this bust."

Video from a drone, traveling at a high rate of speed, showed the rural landscape zip by. In the distance a Moo Station restaurant came into focus.

Chapter 7
Moo Burgers

The street-side sign proudly announced, "Moo Station - Food security for the whole family."

Colin snickered at the irony of "food security" when only Party elites could afford the restaurant's prices. But it wasn't always this way.

The restaurant and its sign were different before they outlawed all cows. Then, the sign had said, "Moo Burger - Meat so juicy, you'll beg for mo." He was a kid then and barely remembered this. None of this was ever discussed today, except in private.

And while in public, Colin had to play the role of The Party man. Except in a few rare times, like now.

He yanked what he called his "Party Tablet" from his lead-lined briefcase and unhooked his wristwatch, leaving both in the glove box of his truck. This would prevent them from tracking his movements and recording his words.

Members' ubiquitous tablets were constantly scanned by The Party for key words spoken or used in Internet searches. They looked for anything they considered seditious or questioning the current Party mantra.

Every Party member was required to have RFID chips inserted in their wrists. This allowed a member entry to all Party-only access points, as well as to pay for goods and services. But The Party also used these to track each member's location and activities.

His fellow Patriots had his chip removed and attached it to a watch, that he called his Party Watch. This allowed him to play Party man when it made sense to do so. He could then step out of that roll and blend in as one of the proles, simply by changing watches. He didn't think The Party tracked the chips all the time as their range was limited. But every time he entered a retail establishment or Party building, their computers would recognize him. With his Party Watch in the car, his Party persona would stay out of contact with the Moo Station computers and therefore Party computers.

In its place, he put on another watch, with a hacked prole's RFID tag. He also had a separate, albeit illegal, tablet that allowed him to stay in contact with fellow Patriots, which was more or less untraceable. With both, he could travel freely without them knowing who he really was, or even caring. If his hacked RFID was scanned, they'd think he was just a common prole. Proles were mostly ignored by The Party because they had little to no power and were easily controlled because of their interdependency and fear of the Party government. It was the Party members who were carefully scrutinized. For this reason, he did not want The Party knowing that he was going to the illegal part of the restaurant.

Finally, he exited his truck, closing his door behind him. He would have to leave his truck unlocked because his RFID tag usually did this automatically, but it remained in the truck's glove box. He wasn't too worried about someone stealing anything. Theft of a Party vehicle was immediately punishable by several months in a VETC facility. If anyone from The Party was monitoring him, or a Community Patrol drone happened by, they would assume he was taking a nap.

Best to get inside before I'm identified without my Party locators.

As he marched toward the restaurant entrance, he thought about how Moo Stations came to be.

Few restaurants were left, as regular proles couldn't afford to eat out. The costs were astronomical for almost everyone, with federal minimum wage at over six-figures and costs for all ingredients up triple-digits each year. However, Party members were afforded certain benefits, which included receiving enough income for them to afford meals at Moo Stations. It was where they hung out.

Every Moo Station was the same. You had to walk through their Educational Center, before even getting to an ordering kiosk. As you processed through, you'd learn the story of Moo Burger's transformation into Moo Station.

Once inside, he read each display as if he'd never done it before.

At one time, this was a successful franchise of gourmet burger joints. Until, it would seem, its owner, Noel Franklin became woke to the dangers cow flatulence posed to the environment. He then eliminated cow meat and anything else from its menu thought unsavory to Leftist taste buds.

After this, the world-wide ban of cows occurred—*no coincidence there*. Today, for most people, except those few who studied them in labs, cows were just a memory, if even that. And so were all meat-products, now replaced with tasteless plant-based foods, especially multiple derivations of the soy plant.

Noel was well ahead of the curve. To everyone—*only a few knew the real story*—he appeared to have swapped out his cattle and dairy operations with his soy growing and processing. But this was all on the public side, all the while he continued raising cattle, literally in the cavernous basements of Abound's buildings. To the public, and therefore The Party, he was a leader, revered by everyone in The Party. While at the same time, he was also one of the leaders of the Patriots and their plans to revolt against The Party. *It was brilliant*, Colin thought.

He chuckled at two kids pointing to the life-sized hologram of the cows, chewing cud, and one seemingly mooing directly at them. The little girl studied the cow and reached out to touch it, her hand slicing through the moving holographic image.

As far as Colin could tell, this was the only way anyone could learn about the animal. But there was something missing.

In the past, Moo Stations had a cow fart display to demonstrate how bad their flatulence smelled, and to provide a reminder of why they had to be eliminated. But this became more of a side show, as kids would try to double-dog dare each other to withstand multiple doses of cow farts. It didn't last too long as patrons complained about the noise from the kids, and more so, the smell that they had to walk through to get to the restaurant. Some even claimed they had sustained injury from the smell...

Was that even possible? He wondered. *Maybe their cultured noses couldn't handle it anymore.*

"Mommy, how come we don't have cows in the zoo?" the little girl asked. Colin thought it was a good question.

"Because they'll kill you with their farts, stupid," the boy replied. They both wore the same androgynous baggy outfits, with similar blue colored haircuts. Had it not been for the girl's more delicate features, he wouldn't have been able to tell their sexes apart. Of course, with two-hundred declared genders, he couldn't blame parents for going non-descriptive. Who knows whose sensibilities you'd offend now a days? And if you did, you could be brought up for a gender hate crime. Best to be neutral.

The girl glared at what Colin guessed was her brother, pursed her lips, like she was going to spew some angry-laced retort. Instead, she curled her fist and, in one swift motion, punched the boy in the face.

"Time out kids," hollered one of the two men accompanying the kids. Like the kids, each man was dressed in similar androgynous outfits, as well as similar blue hairdos. It would have been creepy if it weren't so common among Party families.

"Come on kids," said the other, "Papa Tom is going to get you the biggest soy-burger they make." Papa Tom snagged the arm of the boy, who was rubbing his face where his sister hit him and contemplating whether or not he should cry.

The first man didn't say anything. He grabbed the little girl's hand, who now wore a proud smile, and they followed.

Colin gave the girl a thumbs up as she was led away.

He watched them as he stepped through the cow hologram and headed to the area where the ordering kiosks were located. He couldn't help but admire that little girl, who one day might become a Patriot. She was already questioning things. Of course, she was a rarity in a world where kids were rewarded more for being subservient to the state and not talking out loud against anything The Party said. Surely, they would indoctrinate this child to comply with Party norms, or send her to a VETC to get "reeducated" if she didn't. Colin held out hope that she'd continue to resist.

He stepped around the bank of ordering kiosks where customers placed their orders, swiped their wrists to pay, and received their meals almost instantly. He read somewhere that soy products had the shelf life akin to that of a Twinkie. So who knew how long they had been prepared and waited delivery via one of the machines. The boy and girl with the two fathers, occupied one. Papa Tom was telling it each item in their order. The Kiosk displayed the item, followed by the price: Soy Supreme Leader... $390; Kelp Khrushchev Krispies... $290; and so on. Their total was already north of $2500 when Colin passed them. The girl was still asking questions. "Go get 'em kid," Colin whispered.

At a door, marked Authorized Personal Only, next to the automated restroom door, Colin gave a quick look around before he swiped his Patriot watch at a black pad. The lock switched green and he entered.

This was the employee entrance, although he had never seen an employee, and wasn't sure one existed on the premises. Like Noel's other operations, this one was nearly fully automated. All the ingredients were transported to each location via self-driving EV trucks and were automatically fed into hoppers in the back of the restaurant. Machines and robots did the rest: from preparing the food to cleaning up after everyone left.

A long hallway, with several doors he'd never been in, ended at the Supply Closet. Colin entered, as if he were casually going to grab some "supplies". He switched on the light and closed the door behind him. On a keypad, he typed in the code "1776" and the whole room shuttered and moved.

Down.

He could feel the room descend one long floor, though he had no proof of it. The few supplies on shelves shuttered as they had come to a stop. He opened the door to a din of voices. *Happy voices,* he thought. Unlike the upstairs Party-approved restaurant where everyone spoke quietly, this place was rocking with conversations and joy.

"Hey Colin," someone called him from the center of the large dining area.

He glanced around for its origin and saw Leon, a long-time friend, though a few years younger. Leon sat at one of the dozen or so tables and chewed a thick meat-burger, with its juices pouring out of his mouth, down an elbow and all over his plate.

Colin's own mouth watered just thinking about what he would get on his own burger.

Not yet seeing Noel, he scanned the restaurant to see who else was there that he might know. His eyes found Robert Buford, sporting his infamous long gray mane and equally long gray beard. He'd never met the man, but he was legendary in Patriot circles. Colin so wanted to sit down with Buford and ask him questions. If he sat with Buford when Noel came in, perhaps he'd learn even more about what the Cow Fart Apocalypse was really about.

"Yo, Colin," yelled Leon, who was waving so much Colin feared he might fly out of his seat.

He would sit with Leon until Noel arrived. *If he arrived.*

He waved back at Leon and started walking his way, when a pop-sound erupted and an exit door burst open, letting in bright sunlight from above and Enforcers in their black riot gear with ReAD stenciled on their chests. Dozens of them poured inside, one of them yelling, "You are all under arrest, under ReAD orders! Do not move!"

Chapter 8

A free re-education for everyone

"I remember when they were Moo Burgers." AOC mumbled to nobody, while chewing on a new supply of soy candies. She didn't dare mention that she loved their meat burgers, as she was the one who pushed to make them illegal.

She glared at the Picture Screen on the wall a few feet away. It displayed a map of Washington, DC. Although nothing moved, she reminded herself that someone was always watching. The Party referred to this person or people as 'Big Brother,' but she understood *that* was all related to their favorite book, *1984*. Or so she was told.

Could there really be a Big Brother, now? She wondered.

A clatter at the front of the Situational Room drew her attention to HRC's arrival to the meeting and the dozen screens showing various angles of the operation at the Moo Station restaurant.

The main screen showed a group of armored box trucks and a bus backed up around a barn-like structure, below and next to the Moo Station restaurant. Armed men in ReAD uniforms were escorting people from the barn structure into the bus.

"O-ay, I..." AOC held up a forefinger and chewed vigorously at her mouthful and swallowed, before beginning again. "Okay, I have a question. I thought Moo Burgers were no more and they now served only soy burgers. Did they change back? And what's with that old barn?"

"I got this," KH said and stepped in front of the general who had been explaining the details of their operation to arrest the patrons and workers of the suspected meat burger joint, run below and behind the Moo Station.

"You see, Missy President, this is another example of illegal activity by that domestic terrorist organization known as the Patriots. They were running an illegal meat burger operation out of the original barn that was one of the first Moo Burger restaurants. They have been doing this the whole time, under the noses of the owner of Moo Station."

"Wow, that's pretty brazen of the Patriots. How did we find this out?"

"We have someone on the inside, who is joining us right now." KH turned to look at the big screen behind her. There, the familiar face of an older black man smiled back at them. He looked like Party elite with his tightly trimmed white hair and beard and designer glasses. "This is Noel Franklin, the CEO of Moo Station. He contacted us earlier and let us know about this illegal operation. Today, he let us know that the infamous fugitive, Robert Buford would be there to meet him. He was instrumental in this bust."

"Hello NF. Thank you for your help in catching these evil terrorists," AOC beamed.

"Hello Missy President. It's my honor to work with you." Noel stated, smiling the whole time.

"How horrible it must have been to find out an illegal operation was being operated on your property?"

"It wasn't so bad, Missy President. We leased to this group a few months ago. They claimed they would be selling vegetables from local co-ops. But my people verified this wasn't the case. Once I knew, I contacted ReAD and worked with them to bring these terrorists to justice."

"So, where's da beef? AOC asked, laughing at her own joke.

"Sorry, Missy President," NF looked like he was holding back laughter and then asked, "What do you mean?"

"Like, with cows being illegal and stuff, how'd they get the beef?"

"Missy President," one of the many military people stood up from her seat. "Major Pat Dandrich, Missy President. I worked with Mr. Franklin on this. We tracked the shipments of beef from Mexico."

"Really?" AOC tilted her head and gave an incredulous look, then straightened up. "Shouldn't we declare war on Mexico then?"

HRC laughed and walked to the front of the room. "MP, Mexico supplies us with all of our cheap labor. It's part of our payoff to their government for keeping their population poor enough so they want to flock to the US illegally. Then we can take advantage of their situation by hiring them for way below minimum wage. All the while getting their votes. No, we don't want to go to war with them."

"Well then who do we blame?"

"It's the cartels, Missy President," Major Pat stated.

KH jumped in again. "After we made all drugs legal, as part of our effort to keep our population controlled, the cartels switched to the illegal cow trade."

AOC grinned wide and jumped from her chair, clapping her hands rapidly. "Great! Can we at least nuke the cartels?"

"No, Missy President," added Major Pat. "We can't use nukes on Mexico soil. But the Mexican government promised they would take care of it for us."

"Damn! You people never let me have any fun." She pouted. "Fine." AOC fell back into her chair, her eyes darted around the room to find something that would be of more interest. They came to rest on a bank of screens that had several news channels always playing. The volume was down on each, but she could see the rolling words. One screen was the CCPN channel, and it had some pulsating graphic that announced, "Cow Fart Apocalypse." A shaky video appeared of the brown fart cloud. "Does this have anything to do with the cow fart apocalypse?" she asked.

"Well, that's also why we're working with the Mexicans," HRC explained. "We're trying to find out if the cartels are colluding with the Patriots."

"Fine. Hil, just tell me, is it time for us to evacuate yet? I think I'd like to see the bunker now."

"It's not time, MP. If the cloud comes here, we'll head to the bunker."

"Okay."

AOC sat back in her comfy fake leather chair in the Situation Room. She huffed out a breath, grabbed a few more candies and tossed them in her mouth. She was told repeatedly, The Party would take care of her, if she followed their orders. She looked back at the Moo Station video on the main screen.

It showed the trucks leading the bus away from the restaurant.

"So, what happens to them? Do they at least go to a firing squad?" She pictured each of the people with blind folds, up against an old brick wall, smoking an illegal cigarette. She wondered when she would get to witness one of these sometime. *Soon*, she hoped.

"No MP," answered HRC. "They're going to one of our VETC's, where they'll have their brains retrained to become loyal Party members and give up their traitorous ways."

"So, no one gets shot?"

"No!"

"How about that B-guy... You know their leader that NF ratted out. He gets shot, right?"

"No. We're going to waterboard him to give up his fellow Patriots. Then he'll be retrained at a VETC."

"Waterboard? That sounds like fun. Can I watch that?"

"No, MP."

"And besides," KH spoke up, "It's time for you to meet with your ReAD committee and attend the book burning celebration. Come on, Missy President."

AOC yawned.

Chapter 9

Time to don your Green and Gold!

The road sign read, "Don your green and gold! You're in George Mason territory."

"Patriots brave and bold!" exclaimed a gruff voice beside him.

Colin turned his head to see it was Robert Buford. "Sorry, I don't understand."

"It's from the George Mason fight song...

> *"Hail to George Mason!*
> *Don your Green and Gold!*
> *We're going to sing for George Mason,*
> *Patriots brave and bold!*
> *And we'll FIGHT! FIGHT! FIGHT!*
> *As we march onward to victory!"*

The last line Buford practically yelled, drawing the eyes of the rest of the bus' occupants.

"Shut up back there!" hollered someone from the front of the bus.

Buford tossed a glare in that direction before continuing, "It's appropriate for Patriots of today," he said in a measured tone, though still just as gruff. Buford leaned into Colin's ear and whispered, "Be ready, son. We won't be here long." Then he sat back, turned his head to the left and stared out the same window Colin had been looking through.

It had been roughly a twenty-minute trip from when they had been arrested to when they drove through the first campus gate of George Mason University.

This was not at all what Colin had expected.

He figured they were being taken to some sort of prison-like facility, with cells, where they'd be subjected to all sorts of unspeakable torture. He certainly didn't think the VETC facilities were actually universities.

At a turn in the road, he saw the giant fence. And the guards.

Standing at least ten feet tall and crowned with razor wire, a fence stretched out as far as he could see from both sides of a double gate, blocking their entrance. From a small guard house, just outside the fence, an armed VETC guard popped out. The man gave their bus a stare and then made a circular motion with a fist and the gate rolled open.

The bus slowed until there was enough room for them and the guard waved them through.

As they passed through the gate, the facility looked more like the prison he had expected, and not what was once an actual liberal arts university.

Only a few moments later, they squealed to a stop. The bus' rear doors were flung open. An armed ReAD Enforcer ordered the detainees to stand up and file out of the bus.

They marched off the bus and toward a large building up ahead. Although a sparce number of their group mumbled a few words, most of his fellow detainees muzzled themselves. No doubt they were as anxious as he was about what lay ahead for them.

"Don't worry, kid," said Buford from behind. "You'll be fine. Just stick close to me."

"Thanks, sir," Colin whispered.

"Shit, kid. I ain't in the Army. You can call me Bob."

"Thanks, Bob," Colin responded, in a voice that quavered.

They processed through an open doorway of the building, above which a temporary banner was hung. The material was distressed-looking, as if it were exposed to several seasons of Virginia weather. The banner read, "GMU VETC." Colin knew this stood for Vocational Educational & Training Center, which sounded less threatening than "reeducation center."

Inside, it looked more like a gymnasium.

On the far wall stretched a neglected banner proclaiming, "George Mason Patriots" beside a logo of a rifle crossed against a sword. One of its four corners had become detached and curled over the other.

Buford laughed from behind him.

Colin also recognized both the humor and the irony. They were suspected members of a group called the Patriots, who were just forcibly sent to a former university, which honored the country's founding patriots of the past, so they could be reeducated into a manner of thinking, which was completely contrary to what the country was founded on. It was like their forefathers were cheering them on and their captors were either too lazy or too full of their own rhetoric to remove these overt pro-Patriot messages.

The gym already contained maybe twenty other detainees seated inside a chain link fenced-in area, thrown together in the center of what was once GMU's basketball court. As their group was being led inside the fenced area, Colin glanced back and counted thirty members among their group. This struck him as wrong.

The group of people already detained were from someplace else; probably other suspected

Patriots The Party had rounded up. They were not part of his group. His best guess was that the black-market burger place had, at the most, maybe twenty patrons inside. There couldn't be more than two or three staff members. He couldn't account for the others.

Also, interesting was that based on the hundred or so seats in the area, he guessed they were continually processing people from different locations and raids. Otherwise, they would be overflowing with people in no time. So this was just a holding pen.

They were led to the open seats behind the existing group, some of whom turned to look at Colin's group, whispering to each other. A few pointed in his direction. When Colin sat down, Buford sat next to him. He realized it was Buford who drew their attention. He wondered if was just his luck that Buford was parked beside him or something more.

"I understand you're a favorite of Noel's," Buford whispered.

"You know No...? Of course, you do. You said we would be fine. But how could you know this?" Colin asked, keeping his head pointed forward, making every attempt to keep his voice at whisper-level, too.

"Because this is my second time here."

Colin couldn't help it. He turned to face Buford, who was smiling at him. "But..." Colin sputtered. It was a mystery why this man would allow himself to be in a position to be caught again... Then it hit him: Buford was here on purpose; he knew he was going to be arrested; and he knew who Colin was through Noel. It all made sense. It had also gnawed at him to this point, that Noel was conspicuously absent from the restaurant when they were arrested, even though Noel had told him to not rush over there. Noel *had known* the bust was going to happen.

Colin glared at Buford. The man's smile was even larger than before. He'd been watching Colin's face the whole time, waiting for him to work through the scenario. "I can see you get it now. Noel was right about you." Buford leaned closer, held a hand over his mouth and said something barely above the sound of a breath, "We have a few minutes before it happens and Noel said you had questions. So, let's talk."

Colin was flabbergasted that this icon of their party was singling him out to answer his questions. And yet he also felt acutely aware that others were looking their way. There was a growing chatter in the building. He raised his voice just a little, while doing what Buford had done, shielding his mouth with his hand. "Thanks... Bob. I'm honored. But don't the walls of this place have ears?"

"No worries, Colin. If we talk this way, The Party won't hear us and neither will any of the spies in our group?"

"Spies?" Colin hadn't even considered this.

"Surely you noticed more people in our group than were in and worked at the restaurant? The Party is renowned for mixing in spies with new groups, to infiltrate those groups. No doubt, several of those in front of us or behind of us now are trying to listen to us. That's why they put us in this holding area. After a few hours, they'll interview each of us individually and compare notes with their spies."

Colin couldn't restrain himself. Although he had kept his head pointed forward most of the time, his eyes darted around, scrutinizing the heads and faces of each of his fellow detainees. Sure enough, two of those heads were staring at them, scrutinizing them back.

"Again, thanks. I'm curious about this place. The university being used as a reeducation center? And, what do they plan to do with us? The rumor going around is that they electroshock you until you're a drooling idiot."

Buford guffawed, though he kept his mouth covered until it passed a few seconds later. "Not quite. You see, GMU *was* a Leftist University. They did such a good job indoctrinating regular students, The Party devised a plan to indoctrinate Conservatives who didn't tow The Party line. This is the idea that grew into the VETC. There are now hundreds of them all over the USTP."

"USTP?"

"United States of The Party! It's what they secretly call our country now."

Colin shook his head. "So, what do they have planned for us, intense classes on gender study?"

"You're actually pretty close. We will be forced to watch porn, episodes of Real Housewives—a reality TV show from years past, and CCPN TV… All-day-long. They'll force us to take classes such as All White People Must Die, My 5000 Genders, A Baby Begins When We Tell You, and Communists Are Your Friends. They'll keep pressing and pressing, until we conform."

Buford removed his hand from his mouth., "It's not far off," he said loudly enough to antagonize those who were scrutinizing their words, "from what Leftist students of the past consumed when they turned into what became BLM and other radicals who took over our country."

"So, how did you get out the first time?" Colin whispered, still keeping his mouth covered.

Buford did the same. "I have someone on the inside."

Colin nodded.

An alarm blared, like a fire alarm, cutting off all conversation.

"It will happen soon, son," Buford said. "You're going to smell the stink first and you'll feel faint. Don't worry, it's all part of the process. Just get down on the floor so you don't hit your head. When you wake up, everything will be fine."

The alarm continued to blare and the conversations grew louder to be heard over the alarm.

But there was something else.

A few of the voices asked questions like, "What is that?" or "Do you smell that?"

Then Colin did as well.

It smelled like... Cow flatulence! He recognized it immediately.

But unlike his times at one of Noel's facilities, he now felt lightheaded.

Buford was already on his knees. Colin followed suit.

He thought of the banner's saying, "*Patriots brave and bold!*" and then everything went dark.

Chapter 10

At what temperature does digital paper burn?

AOC glanced at the tablet just handed her. It contained a long list of books slated to be destroyed, supposedly for inciting hate speech.

"Please follow me to the book burning ceremony," KH insisted and led the way out of the Situation Room. HRC stayed behind.

Just before the door closed behind AOC, she overheard HRC address the generals, pleading with them to not wait any longer to go to the bunker. *Now, AOC was getting nervous.*

In the hallway, KH turned and said, "So, Missy P, the book burning ceremony will be broadcast as if it were being held on the White House North Lawn."

AOC glared at her. "Does that make sense; you know with the fart cloud approaching?" She thought about also mentioning what she'd just heard but didn't want to alarm KH more than she already was.

"Oh no, it's not really being held there. We're doing this, with the members of my committee, in one of the green rooms, making it look like it's on the North Lawn. It will then be broadcast later."

"Oh, okay." AOC thought about this a moment longer, before returning her attention to the list on the tablet. "So, *all* of these books are being burned?" AOC scrolled through several pages of the list on the tablet. "There are so many."

"First off, they're not literally going to be burned, because there are no more paper books. Remember, they don't exist, except in Party-member homes or museums because paper products are illegal." KH glanced at AOC and saw she was losing her attention.

"We simply delete them from the publishing platforms that sell them on the Internet. And then we go directly into the author's computer and remove it from there. Finally, we remove it from every laptop, tablet and eReader on earth."

"Wait, what about the right to privacy? Isn't that protected or something?" She looked up to the ceiling, and then smiled. "You know, like when the Feds accidentally found animal porn on a Party member's computer, but they had to return it because of privacy rights?"

"Ah, that story was false... And ahhh, this is totally different Missy P." She cleared her throat and straightened her blouse. KH looked back up at AOC. "Ah, you see, eBooks are not anyone's property. You only buy a license to the book when you purchase a copy. That way there's no ownership of the book, so we inform the publishing platform that sold the book, like Big River, to just remove it.   They have to comply, because as you know, we can do anything under Hate Crimes Law."

AOC nodded her acknowledgment.

"So, when we're done, every copy that was ever created is wiped away, as if it never existed before."

"But why get rid of *every* copy?"

"Because it's seditious. Remember, it all started with the Bible. We canceled that because of all of its violence toward people of color, hate toward the LGB Etc. communities, cruelty toward the environment, and total lack of inclusion for anyone who didn't believe what Christians believe. Plus, every week, it incited riots at places called churches."

"I remember those. They had sing-a-longs with the band leader they called a pastor." She smiled at her ability to recall this long forgotten tidbit of knowledge. "Now, remind me about the Muslims? Why do they get to keep their Korman?"

"You mean Koran. That's because of an agreement we made with Middle Eastern countries. If they don't bomb us, we would let Muslims keep their book."

AOC considered this. The Party was constantly making deals with different groups, so she guessed it made sense.

"But then, we found more and more hate-speak in fictional works, so we targeted those authors and their books. Every week, my committee chooses the books we would quote-unquote, burn"—she made air quotes with her fingers.

"What I don't understand is how do you do it... You know, remove a copy from someone's computer?"

"Well, it's technical. Essentially every computer and device has a Party program required to be included that allows us to control and monitor it, as well as every website server. When we want to eliminate a book, we target the name and title. Then everything on every computer or device with that title and author's name is removed forever. It's like that author's book never existed in the first place."

AOC nodded at this and then noticed she had been led by KH to a door with F451 stenciled on it.

When KH opened the door, she noticed the small room didn't have one stick of furniture inside. It was completely green, from floor to ceiling. "Thank me lucky charms," she blurted along with a storm of giggles.

"Right. That's funny Missy P. You're so witty." KH cackled along with AOC. But her braying grew to such a high pitch that AOC had to shield her ears and step into the room.

Once inside, she saw others in the room, standing back, waiting for them. In the middle was a big black "X" on the floor.

"I get it," AOC stated. "So, we pretend that we're like burning paper books in the middle, right?"

"Exactly, the geniuses at the CCP will make it look like we're having a bonfire on the White House North Lawn."

"Okay, that sounds so cool. I can't wait to see it on CCPN. Let me see again who is on our list to be cancelled this week."

"Hey, Stephen Queen. Oh, I like his movies. Why him?"

"At first the party didn't like him because his books were too long, meaning a lot of paper had to be used. But after paper was eliminated, he left The Party in protest."

"No wonder I don't see any more of his movies."

"So, will he have to go to one of the reeducation..."—AOC yawned—"thingies?"

"We use the same term as the Chinese Communist Party, Vocational Education and Training Centers or Vet-C. He's already there, although taking a longer time to get reeducated than other authors.

"And don't worry." KH leaned over to AOC's ear and whispered. "We won't cancel all of his books. We actually keep copies of his and other popular books that you or Party members want in the Party library, which is available only to Party Elites. They will just be eliminated from everywhere else."

AOC tried to imagine what a digital Party library would look like. She noticed KH and the others were glaring at her. "That's okay, KH. I don't read books anymore; they're too long." She yawned again.

KH whispered, "You're almost done Missy P. Remember, POTUS duties end at 12 Noon, per the *Old Joe Rule* we set up, in honor of the world's oldest president."

"Of course, I remember him. He was the one who kept sniffing my hair at conferences. So, he's why we all stop work at 12?" She asked this to herself, mostly.

"Shall we finish?" KH insisted.

"Oh, yes. What do I do?"

"Just read the words on the screen there," KH pointed to the large TV screen on the farthest wall, already displaying text. AOC saw the red light above it, which told her the camera was not on yet.

"When the screen says it, I introduce you to the members of the committee," KH ushered the group forward. "Oh, and here are your matches." KH handed AOC a box of matches.

She accepted the box, but her face twisted as she opened up the little drawer inside.

"Just grab one of those sticks and strike it to the rough surface on the side of the box. Nothing will happen, but it will look like you've struck a real match. Then toss it onto the floor, where you see the big "X".. The real fun happens when it's broadcast on TV

KH looked at the committee members for confirmation and then at AOC.

"Okay are you ready to record?"

Chapter 11

Reprogramming rule reversal

Colin opened his eyes to find Buford standing over him, offering a hand.

"Time to get up, Patriot, and start the new revolution," he said from a fog above. Buford's hand provided the necessary stability to stand.

"How long?" Colin asked. He was going to ask *how long he'd been out*, but that's all that came out. As soon as he said this, the soupy thoughts in his head cleared and he could concentrate, as if whatever zapped him had never happened.

"Only a few seconds. It packs a wallop, don't it?"

"What... What was that?"

"That, my friend is what The Party is calling a 'toxic cow fart cloud,' but it was no natural phenomenon and it's not toxic... Except to some people's way of thinking."

A flood of questions swamped Colin's mind, but he remembered the 'spies' Buford had warned him about, just before they were knocked out. His eyes darted around their enclosure and scrutinized every man and woman. Each appeared to be in a similar position: picking themselves off the floor. Only a few looked as clear-headed as Buford, and now Colin. Others appeared as dazed as he was, before the fog cleared. No one seemed interested in the two of them now.

Colin whispered, "Shouldn't we still watch what we say here?"

Buford ignored Colin's question, already stepping over a chair in front of them to help up one of the two women, who had been scrutinizing them so overtly. She had been face down on the floor moments ago. Buford said to her in a very caring voice, "You're gonna be confused for a few hours, but then the world will start to make sense again, and you will start to feel some joy. Welcome back, Patriot."

He returned to face Colin, "Not to worry about what you say. Everyone here is now a friend."

Colin cast his own confused glance and was about to ask what Buford meant by this, when Buford turned the other way and was now headed to the secured gate entrance of their enclosure. Concurrently, a VETC guard was approaching the same point from the gym's opening outside.

There was no alarm between either man. Instead, they were like two friends eagerly meeting at the fence line, to chat about the weather or each other's family.

When the guard arrived at the enclosure's entrance, without any hesitation he unlocked the padlock, and swung open the gate. The two men first clasped hands and then each other, like they were brothers. This must have been the "inside" man Buford spoke about.

Buford faced the entire group from the gate. "Come on, Patriots, one and all. It's time to leave and take back our country."

The woman Buford had helped up, spoke to the other suspected spy, who had occupied the seat next to her, "Hear that? Again, he called us Patriots. And though my brain is screaming that that term is evil, it doesn't feel like it now."

"What day is it?" asked the other.

"Colin, come on," hollered Buford from the fence opening.

Colin double-timed it to where his fellow detainees were starting to stream out.

"Colin, follow me," Buford instructed. His friend, the guard was already gone. Perhaps the man was instructed to check on the other guards.

It took some effort to keep up with Buford, a man at least twice his age, who had already disappeared out the gym doorway.

Once outside, Colin saw several of the armed VETC guards looking their way and he immediately ducked behind a large hedge. But only for a moment.

Buford continued, not even flinching, and trotted past the guards He headed toward the parked ReAD bus and its driver. The same one who had delivered them to GMU.

Colin found himself standing up straight as a board, unable to avert his gawking at the surreal site before him.

There were a dozen or so guards outside, scattered around the grounds. Some still appeared unconscious, others barely awake and slowly rising, while the remaining four that Buford had walked past looked like zombies. They were standing in place, but it was as if they had no brain functions to tell them what to do next. They just stared forward, without reacting to what they saw.

Buford approached the driver, who was sitting against the bus' front bumper. This man had also been staring at nothing, as if in a trance, totally oblivious to Buford's presence. Buford spoke into the driver's ear, and then handed the driver a slip of paper. The driver examined the paper, nodded, stood up and disappeared into its interior. It was like a robot who had just received its programing.

The bus' gasoline engine fired up and the driver appeared to be preparing to move. Buford stepped away and marched over to the four zombie-like guards who were still standing in their own mental fog.

He walked right up to the group, unafraid that they would recall the parameters of their job to detain and lock him up. Buford spoke to the group. Colin was too far away to hear what he was saying, and he couldn't even guess. But like the bus driver, he gave all four instructions. Buford pointed to the sky and each of the guard's heads tilted upward.

Colin giggled with incredulity at this, and then gasped at what happened next.

Buford grabbed the rifle from the nearest guard, who let it go without the slightest protest, and made a demonstration of shooting at the sky. All four guards nodded, as if they too had just accepted their new programming. Buford handed the rifle back to the guard before finally trotting back toward the gym.

Buford knew all of this was going to happen or he was behind it.

As Colin waited Buford's return to drill him with even more questions, he was startled to see the entire group of detainees had collected around him. A few were talking to each other now, including his friend Joel, whom after all the commotion he'd forgotten about. They were asking each other many of the same questions Colin had.

Buford stopped a few feet from Colin, but addressed the group. "Can I have your attention, my fellow Patriots?"

The group fell silent, just as their bus screeched to a halt behind Buford.

"The bus that brought us here will take you to a place where others like us have come together. Once there, you will get all of your questions answered. Until then, please get on the bus and be patient until you get to your destination."

The driver was already out of the bus and ushering them inside.

"Go on now," Buford instructed.

Shockingly, every person quietly formed into a single-file line and made their way into the bus.

Colin, who had been witnessing all of this slack-jawed, barely registered Buford telling him to, "Follow me."

Colin snapped his mouth shut and followed. From behind he volleyed some of his questions: "What the hell was all that? How did you do that? What were you saying to those—"

"Hang on, Hoss. We don't have much time. I need your help and then I'll explain everything."

Colin scampered to keep up.

"At least tell me where we're going right now?"

"We're going to collect a few of the top Patriots who have been locked away for a while. It's the main reason why I got myself arrested and placed here."

Buford increased his pace, now almost running But Colin kept abreast of him, matching his stride, not wanting to miss anything the man was willing to share.

"Okay, I'll bite, like whom?"

Buford didn't answer as he glanced at the dormitory they were passing. He pointed to the building next to it.

Colin looked that way. The second building was much nicer looking and bigger. The sign at the top of the building stood out among all the others. It was the most ostentatious of all signs of any on campus that he had seen so far. When he read it, he instantly understood why.

In big bold lettering, it read, "TRUMP FAMILY DORMITORY"

"Are you shitting me?"

Chapter 12
Let's get this party started

The head-thumping music finally made AOC feel at ease, just as rain drops on a rooftop might soothe the souls of others.

"I want another!" hollered IO over the music. She flashed a smile and then almost fell over, an elbow the only thing keeping her from finding the floor.

That would make it like ten shots of tequila for someone who declared herself a faithful Muslim. *Isn't this sacrilege?* AOC thought and then laughed, remembering this woman married her brother, just to help him get citizenship years ago.

At least IO believes in something, AOC considered.

She didn't believe in anything. Not really. She often questioned her own faith to The Party, in spite of all that it did for her. And that made her feel guilty at being so judgmental. "I want one, too," RT blared and pounded the bar with a balled up fist.

"Okay, one more round for everybody!" proclaimed AOC.

The entrance door to what used to be called the Queen's Bedroom, slowly opened half-way. An elderly-looking man with deep bags under his eyes and wearing rumpled pajamas stuck his head in and flashed his perverted smile.

AOC clicked down the volume on the sound system to hear what the creepy man had to say.

In a grainy but familiar voice, "Hi girls. Can I have one?"

"Go to bed!" someone hollered and threw a shot glass at the door, narrowly missing the 42nd President's head by mere inches.

He ducked away into the hallway, pulling the door closed behind him.

"I feel bad for the old guy," said RT. "I mean he's been relegated to the Lincoln Bedroom, while his wife is in the President's Bedroom... Hey, AOC why isn't that your bedroom?"

AOC just grinned to cover her true feelings. She may have been given the smallest bedroom in all of the White House, but she received other perks instead. For one, she had this private bar. "Besides, HRH"—she thought about it for a moment—"Ha! It's not Her Royal Highness, I meant, HRC always wanted the Presidency, but never got it..." Her addled thoughts were sidetracked easily.

"No HRH is more correct," someone said.

AOC grinned wider and clicked up the volume of the music, even though she knew that the Lincoln Bedroom was across the hall from them. Mostly, she just wanted to drown out the ongoing argument between AP, another squadron member who looked just as angry as ever, and RFO on the other side of the bar.

RFO was the newest member of their squadron. Some still called her Vato, before she identified as one of the female genders. That was when she was a he who had taken on a Mexican-sounding name when first running for and then losing the Senate. Recently, she had identified as a female person of color. "What-ya mean, yo got yo reparations check already?" RFO pleaded with both of her arms churning the air. "I identified as a female person of color just befo da new law. So, I should be in da system."

"Listen you punk-ass bitch," screamed AP.

RFO burst into tears, just like AOC had taught her and shrunk away from the shorter, but much scarier-looking woman.

At first, AP wasn't buying RFO's tears. But then AP allowed her shoulders to slump—maybe so she didn't seem like a total bully—and in a lower, more compassionate voice, almost drowned out by the music, she said, "Sorry, Vato, I didn't mean—"

"—It's Reyanna now," RFO cut in.

"Whatever," AP replied. "You know it's a new program, and it's hard for The Party to print money as fast as everyone is using it. Plus, those who were assigned as persons of color at birth had first priority, over those who are trans-colored."

AOC thought that way of thinking sounded biased but didn't dare say anything out loud, not wanting to be the focus of AP's ire.

RFO/Vato/Reyanna seemed to accept this and meekly directed a gaze at AOC. "You look pretty in that outfit."

"Thanks, Vato," AOC said, looking away and then back, horrified at what she had just done. "OMG, I didn't mean to deadname you. I am so sorry."

"No worries, Missy P. Really, I mean it: I just loved how cute that looks on you."

AOC offered a smile, while giving herself a look over in the Picture Screen, currently on its mirror setting. It was the bartender/waitress outfit she had worn years ago. She donned it just to break in the new party digs. "I'll let you borrow it some time."

AOC laughed at the thought of Reyanna's six-foot-four-inch frame in her little outfit.

"Damn girlfrien..." declared CB at the other end of the bar.

AOC turned to look in her direction, just as CB's whole body convulsed backward. Luckily, her fingers, like claws, automatically dug into the bar, preventing her from falling over. "You yook fi in dat oufit." CB's eyes rolled back in her head and then returned their hazy gaze at AOC.

She was as equally plastered as the rest of her friends... Well, except the final member of their squadron, JB, who had been face down on the Andrew Jackson bed after the first shot. *That guy could never hold his liquor.*

That was fine with her. She preferred just the girls breaking in the new bar.

AOC glanced around again at what was formally known in the White House guidebooks as the Queen's Bedroom. That was until she had converted it into her own private nightclub, complete with long bar and sound system. A giant neon sign, above the Picture Screen, blinked, "AOC's Place," which had been just delivered and installed today.

It was her one ask when The Party "requested" she play this role.

Automatically, AOC lined up six shot glasses and skillfully poured the amber colored liquid into equal shots, without needing to measure. *This* was the one job she knew how to do well. And the one job no one told her how to do.

She flashed a glance at the Picture Screen. She didn't care if the Party didn't like it. Though she guessed they probably didn't care, either.

Still, she held up a middle finger at the sign and smiled.

The liquor bottle was set back and the five glasses were slid towards her friends on the other side of the bar.

AOC hoisted her glass in the air. "To the Squadron!" She proclaimed and waited for them to respond.

They called out "The Squadron" in unison and downed their drinks, just as the door flew open.

"Go away, Bill," AP yelled.

This time it wasn't an elderly ex-president, but a studly looking general who bounded inside, looked around and punched the off button on the sound system silencing the loud music.

"Missy President," he boomed, "You are needed in the SitRoom ASAP."

AOC smiled at what looked like two separate men, each with the same broad chests full of medals, beefy shoulders with Air Force patches, and chiseled faces. She knew it was just one... plus a whole lot of tequila. "You want to come in and take a load off, general?"

"Sorry Missy President, but you are needed right away. We have a situation that requires your authorization."

She attempted to focus in on the middle of what now looked like several men, and not get any more nauseous from what felt like the room spinning.

Then, a shocking thought crept up into her muddled mind, *The cow fart cloud! Is it here now?*

She shot sidelong glances at each of her squadron friends. All of them ignoring AOC and the interruption. Each focused on their own little world.

AOC made an attempt to straighten up, put her glass down, and marched out of the room, feeling just a little more sober than she did moments earlier. It didn't last.

Just before the door closed behind her, she heard RFO say, "I'll play bartender now."

She couldn't explain it, but deep down in her hazy mind, she knew it would be the last time she would see them this way.

Chapter 13
Where Patriots go to die

"Is he here?" Colin asked, taken aback at the possibilities of what this may mean: POTUS 45 might actually be here! Palm Beach County had taken over Mar-a-Lago some time ago and kicked him and his family out by using eminent domain. Could The Party have relocated him here? And how did this dormitory, with its big sign, come to be... A huge donation?

"No, but some of his family is and quite a few others you may have heard of," Buford smiled at Colin's expression. "But we don't have a lot of time. That is my inside guy, Fred Serpico," Buford pointed at the door. "Help him get everyone from this dorm onto the large bus we saw in the big parking lot."

The guard Colin had seen earlier unlocking their temporary enclosure in the gym, popped out of the front door of the dormitory building's entrance.

"Wait, where are *you* going?" Colin asked.

"I'm going to get Q," Buford stated plainly, as if he announced he was going to the local Giantmart to get a tub of tofu.

"Wait, you mean *the Q*... of Qanon fame?"

"Yep." Buford had already turned away and was marching toward another dormitory building.

"So, who is it?" Colin yelled out, making sure his question was heard.

Buford gave an indirect glance, only partially arresting a grin that told Colin, 'I know, but I'm not going to tell you.'

"You gonna just stand there or help?" barked Serpico.

Buford, was already halfway to the other building, when he bellowed back, "Get everybody to the big bus within the next five minutes."

"Colin!" Serpico demanded, not hiding the frustration over Colin's inaction.

"Sorry. Coming." Colin hurried into the dorm entrance. He came to an abrupt halt when he saw many familiar faces, and others he didn't recognize, crowded in the foyer and extending up the adjoining stairwell.

Near the top of the stairwell, heading down from the first floor, was Donald Trump Jr. who was leaning forward and whispering something to Lara Trump. She cast a questioning gaze at the clog of people in front of the entry. Each of them had a small suitcase in one hand, while grasping the handrail down with the other.

At the base of the stairwell, Ben Shapiro was chuckling at something that Glenn Beck had said. Shapiro grew more serious and asked a question back in a full-tilt barrage of words that were spoken rapid-fire. Colin missed all but the last three words, "...Patriots will prevail?"

Sean Hannity was busy explaining his reasoning of why they were being released, counting down the list of arguments via his fingers to Alex Jones. Jones seemed more concerned that Colin was staring, gap-mouthed, at both of them. "You got something to add, pal?" Jones demanded of Colin.

"Ah, no Mr. Jones. Just happy to be a part of your rescue."

That seemed to pacify Jones enough that he gave a thumbs up and returned his attention to Hannity, who was on his sixth finger.

Candace Owens had her back to him, standing halfway up the stairwell, while busily explaining to Lou Dobbs and Larry Elder how she'd love to run for the Presidency, if The Party, through Domination Voting Schemes, did not control all the voting in the country.

"It could be aliens behind this." a familiar voice rang out from an unfamiliar face in the group on the ground floor.

"No George, it's just this nice young man,

coming to help us escape the shackles of our bondage," responded Governor Mike Huckabee. Behind him was his daughter, Sarah.

George's voice then clicked in Colin's head, *this was George Noory of late-night radio fame.*

Colin was in the presence of some of the greatest Conservative voices of his generation, and the generation previous to him, and he was going to help them break out of their Party prison. He thought he might just piss himself with excitement.

"Fine, but I know who Big Brother is," stated Noory. "It's Ba—"

"Excuse me, folks," interrupted Serpico, who was hollering from the top of the stairwell. "Our good friend and Patriot, Colin Backwater there"—he pointed at Colin—"is going to show you to a bus that will take you to safety."

All eyes turned to Colin, who felt instantly nervous at the simple responsibility being handed to him. He wondered who was going to drive the bus, how they were going to get it started and where they were going? None of which he knew. In fact, he really didn't know anything that was going on, other than there appeared to be a lot of planning behind it. And behind that planning was Buford and his uncle, Noel.

"God bless you, son," said Huckabee.

Candace Owens, loudly stated, "Today, this is no longer the place where Patriots go to die."

Colin attempted to hold onto his growing smile, even thought he was a bundle of nerves. He tried to stand up tall, but he felt very small, compared to these luminaries.

"Colin," yelled down Serpico, "I'm going to get Prager and Ingraham who are still up here. You go ahead and take this group to the bus."

Colin gave the thumbs up and turned to the group, "Come on everyone. I'll show you your ticket to freedom." *God that sounded stupid*, Colin castigated himself while opening the door and stopped momentarily to hold it open for Anna Paulina Luna, the Florida Congresswoman and Liz Wheeler, the podcaster and former OAN reporter. Both had disappeared several years ago, yet here they were now. "Thanks, young man. Please show us where to go next," Wheeler said, flashing a big smile.

"You rock, Patriot!" said Luna, beaming a smile and a thumbs up.

He mouthed, "You're welcome" to both and started walking.

"Okay everyone, follow me," Colin said, but he took care to walk slowly enough that everyone could keep up with him. They walked in procession out of the dorm, down the private road, which led to the parking area where several vehicles, including a luxury coach came into view.

Halfway up the road, a VETC guard was sitting cross-legged on the pavement, like a statue of Sitting Bull. He wearily gazed up at this group passing him, with that same foggy look plastered all over his face as the other guards. Colin wondered how long this one would take to recover. Some of his group stopped in front of Sitting Bull, seemingly afraid to go any further.

"Don't worry," Colin said, trying to remember what Buford had said earlier. "The guards are our friends now. Please continue to the bus. We're almost there." Colin pointed at the big black bus in the parking lot.

His group gave a wide breath around Sitting Bull as they made their way to a Mercedes tour bus, next to a smaller one. Its doors were already open, beaconing them in.

Colin peaked inside, not sure what he was checking for. He was taken aback when he noticed a bus driver already there, quietly waiting in her seat. She smiled, but didn't say anything. Colin nodded and gave a glance down the luxury coach, with its leather seats. "Damn. How in the hell did you arrange..." He shook his head and stepped out to face the group of Conservative big wigs, all silent and patiently waiting for Colin to give them the okay to climb aboard.

"Looks good," Colin said, keenly aware of his inability to string together anything resembling a smart sentence near these celebrities.

Just then, he caught a glimpse of Buford escorting someone with long thin hair into the smaller version of their bus. He couldn't see this person's face. But, abruptly that person was gone.

"That was Q," Noory yelled out.

"I had no idea," Huckabee said above a whisper.

"And I missed it," Colin cursed quietly.

Buford made haste over from the small bus, hollering, "Come on folks. Everyone get on the bus so we can blow this pop stand."

Colin stepped aside so that the group could board.

Buford brought up the tail of the group.

Colin watched each person board, trying not to grin like a giddy school girl at the Conservative superstars, each of whom stopped to thank *him,* before stepping onto the bus.

When Buford pulled up to Colin, the ladies he had held open the door for earlier jogged up. They had somehow gotten separated from the group, doing what he didn't know. Both were chirpy about something. They restrained themselves before entering the bus.

Congresswoman Luna attempted to confine her amusement with her hand. She removed it when she stepped up, "We had to leave our captors a little message." She said with a chuckle. The reporter, Wheeler, didn't even attempt to hold back her glee, as she bounded up the stairs. Her laughter followed.

Wonder what that was all about.

Serpico walked up to the bus steps and stepped aside, as Laura Ingraham, followed by Dennis Prager approached the bus. They smiled at Colin and mounted the bus steps.

When Buford, Serpico and Colin were the final three, Serpico shook each of their hands and announced, "Going back to get everyone ready for Phase II. See you both later."

"Be well, Fred," Buford offered.

Serpico turned and scampered away.

"You did good, Colin," Buford said, offering to shake his hand.

Colin didn't think he did anything special, except show up. Still, he returned the handshake.

They stopped when they heard the buzz of CP drones in the air.

Colin lifted his head to take in the bright sky. At the same time, gunfire erupted. But Colin didn't flinch. He could tell it was not aimed in their direction.

"I'll be damned. They're doing it," Buford exclaimed.

Standing in the road were the four guards Buford had spoken to previously. Each of them were aiming and firing their rifles into the sky at the incoming Community Patrol drones. One by one, the guards were picking off the drones, until the buzzing stopped.

None of it made any sense. "How did you manage all of this..." Colin started to ask, but then bit his tongue.

"Come on Colin, let's get out of here. I'll fill you in on the details once we're on our way."

Chapter 14

Technicolor yawn

"Why aren't we going to the bunker?" AOC cried, after the Air Force general roughly pushed her into the Situation Room. "I don't wanna go here."

"Missy President!" Someone announced to the room. Everyone rose and she felt herself being brought further inside, but didn't feel like she was moving her own feet. At that point, she wasn't sure she could even feel her feet.

AOC glanced downward to confirm this and realized the general's arm was hooked around hers, to lead her to her chair at the other end of the long table.

"Missy P, sorry to interrupt your break but we have a situation here," said HRH—*or was it HRC, she couldn't remember now.*

A moment after that thought, AOC burst into a laughing fit when she remembered what HRH meant. "Her Royal Hiney," she whispered to herself.

That was all it took. She couldn't suppress the hurricane of laughter that followed... Until the big screen flashed a moving drone image, followed by other drone videos on multiple little screens. All the images moving, showing drones blazing over the earth at a high rate of speed. She caught her breath as her laughter was immediately replaced with a queasy feeling.

"Missy President. Can I have your attention?" asked a general—*who was much older than the one who rudely interrupted my party and brought me here.*

Old General stood in front of the main screen. The other screens surrounded him like a crown of seemingly disconnected but continually moving images. Only after a few moments did some of them appear to be of a university campus. But it was all too much. The crazy amount of moving. Too much movement.

AOC looked away from them and focused her attention on the general's hand. He had something in it... it made a laser light on one of the screens.

Damn, even he has a pointer now, she thought. "I want one of those!" she bellowed, then burped.

Old General glared at AOC, casting a mean and disapproving look at her.

Why am I in trouble?

She thought of her drinking party at AOC's Place and tried to remember how much alcohol she had consumed. *Old General would probably spank me if he knew*. She grinned back at the man, like a Cheshire Cat.

"To catch you up Missy President, we've had an incident at one of our VETC's."

"Missy P!" called out her Chief of Staff—*It's H-R-C, you numbskull*. "Over here, Missy P..." Now, she looked like two people—*that's twice as scary!* "VETC stands for Vocational Education and Training Center, where we put Conservatives and others who speak out against The Party. Our VETC's are loosely modeled after the PRC's re-education camps in Xinjiang..."

Wow, that's a mouthful... mouthful... That's it, I could eat a mouthful of my candies, she thought. Her head swung wildly from side to side, scanning every part of the cluttered table, until she finally found her bowl of candies, now half emptied by one of her military dudes. "That's mine!" she brayed.

The man stopped chewing. With his mouth still full, he slid the bowl down to someone who slid it further, until it ended up in front of AOC.

"Sorry, Hil. I forgot what you were sa..." She scooped up a handful and tossed them in her mouth before she finished speaking. She slouched down into her seat, throwing her feet on top of the table's edge.

AOC noticed one of her heels was just hanging on the edge, so she slid her body forward, while chewing away. But when she glanced down and noticed her skirt was hiked up to her belly, she gave it a stiff yank. "Don't want to give these boys a show," she thought out loud. This brought her cheeks to a bright shade of red.

"Missy P!" HRC screeched. "This is important. *Please* pay attention."

AOC yanked her feet off the table and let them drop to the floor with a clunk, sending tremors through her body. She glared back at HRC for being such a continual wet rag to all her fun. She had a small sense of what Bill had to endure every single day.

"As I was saying, our VETC facility at George Mason was hit by an offshoot of the fart cloud and we have received reports of major disturbances there. General?" HRC motioned to Old General, a scowl still etched into his face.

I don't like this man.

The general turned on his laser pointer again and drew a circular motion with its beam onto the big screen. The screen showed video of the countryside rushing by at a rapid speed. "These recordings came in minutes ago. In a moment Missy President, we'll see the aftermath of what the fart cloud did to this campus."

Motion sickness immediately swept over her and she fixed her glaze at the table. Just as suddenly, the candies she was chewing on tasted vile. But she couldn't spit them out and knew that HRC wanted her to see this video. She forced herself to look up again, focusing on the images that weren't moving as much.

Two videos showed a campus parking area with a couple of people lying on the ground. The other screens, also more steady now, revealed similar images of people on the ground.

When she started to wonder if they were all dead, she saw survivors: One of the screens showed people walking in a group, being led to a bus. One of the group then pointed up at the camera, as if they could see her.

"What you're seeing now, Missy President," HRC said—*There were two of her again*—"is video of the worst criminals in our history: people so wicked, they had the boldness to publicly disagreed with The Party and every administration since Old Joe, may Gaia rest his soul..."

Don't puke! She commanded herself.

The main screen switched to a closer view of the four people on the ground. They looked like security guards, with official looking black uniforms like those who worked at the various places she had lived. But, they looked dead. She was about to look away when one of them rose to a knee. He had a rifle. And it looked like he was aiming it directly at her. She almost ducked behind the table edge when something happened... The image was gone.

Another video image showed the same guard, aiming his rifle again at the sky. Then smoke at the end of his rifle. Another one of the screens went black.

"Is he shooting at us?" AOC said, not sure if her words were heard outside her own head.

Since no one answered, she assumed her comments weren't verbalized.

The big screen showed another video image of the same four people in guards' uniforms, all with rifles, and all were firing their weapons. More screens went black, the big screen showed the guards shooting in the air.

The big screen image of the four guards went momentarily sideways, and then corrected. Then it listed the other way. It lurched forward and held. It spun around and around, the landscape becoming a blur as the speed of its rolling increased. It was both falling and spinning: the ground came closer, then a flash of the sky, then the ground, then the sky.

Each revolution caused AOC's stomach to do cartwheels.

Then the ground met the camera and the feed went black.

That's when everything AOC had consumed that day, from the giant tofu salad to her soy shake, and all of the candies came up at once. She tried to turn away from the table and aim at the floor. Instead, she heaved one giant torrent of green-brown vomit across the table, onto the military man holding the nuclear football and finally finding the floor.

She wretched for an uncountable amount of time, oblivious to the curses directed at her. But she also heard the howls. They came from the military man she had thrown up on.

With great effort, she lifted her head up, though she felt more wobbly than ever.

She glanced at the military man, caked in the vileness which had come from her stomach. The man, whose face color matched what had come from her gut, glared back at her with a combo of hatred and panic. Then he spewed onto his own feet.

"Sorry," AOC whispered with effort. She laid her head back against the chair's headrest.

She heard a buzz of activity as a blur of new people cleaned up around her.

"Wait, Missy P," HRC said, in an attempt to arrest AOC's attention back. "General, can you bring up the other video you showed us?"

The general didn't say anything, but using the same device that created the laser light, changed the big screen video to one showing a sign on the ground. It looked painted, and like everything else in front of her, this image was muddy.

But then it became clearer and the image zoomed in. It was a message, painted on the road for the drones to see. The message was pretty clear.

"The Party can EAT MY COOTER!
PATRIOTS"

AOC didn't know whether to laugh or be shocked. Mostly she just wanted to lie down.

"Can you believe how seditious this is?" asked the general rhetorically.

AOC found it hard to keep from falling over in her seat, while several military men had rushed in to clean up around her. The guy with the football was gone. *Hope I don't need that*, she thought.

"Missy P!" HRC screeched and snapped her fingers several times.

AOC attempted to focus on her.

There were more of her now.

"We need your authorization." The multi-cloned HRCs walked toward her, grabbing a tablet midway along the table. The HRCs stepped around the multitude of people working to clean up the mess AOC had made.

Standing before AOC, the HRCs fiddled with the tablet—*there were so many of her now*—and presented it to her with a stylus.

AOC gave a passing glance at the tablet and then the stylus pressed into her hand. Her hand moved along the surface of the tablet...

Everything was a fog.

"Your signature will authorize the government to rescind all rights of Americans who call themselves Patriots, and all who are believed to be associated with Patriots, or anyone who knew a Patriot."

Several of the people around the table stood and clapped.

AOC flopped her head down onto the tablet and passed out.

Chapter 15
The Patriot's plan

"Where are we headed?" Colin asked in a low voice from his front seat. He was well aware that George Noory was behind him, listening to every word they said. And even though there were some scattered conversations around the bus, he knew a few more than Noory were listening, too.

Buford had remained deep in thought since their driver put the bus into gear. He was fixated on the world outside of the bus' windshield. "Someplace safe. Then I'll drop you off," he said without averting his eyes.

Colin expected more information than this. A lot more. But so far, Buford had been very thin on the details. "Fine," Colin huffed, not caring who heard them. "Here are my questions: what the hell is going on and what is Operation Cow Fart?"

The whole bus went silent.

Buford finally turned his head toward Colin and cleared his throat. "Yeah, I promised you some answers. But the others need to know, too." He rose from his seat and did a one-eighty to face all of the passengers.

"Fellow Patriots," he said loud enough that everyone could hear him. "We are part of a group of Americans who have pledged our fortunes, lives, and liberties to fight for this great country. But we have been quietly waiting for the right time to take back the country that we loved and lost in 2020. Though many would argue it was lost long before that."

"Those before us, including most of you, had been warned about the grand plans of Leftists, but most didn't listen, either because of chosen ignorance, or because the plans of Leftists seemed too conspiratorial to a reasoned mind, or because we were all just too busy going about our normal lives. I mean, who had time to watch all the TV news channels or pay attention to everything the Leftists said? So we Americans went about our business, clocking in the hours at work, taking kids to school, watching movies and spending time with friends or family.

"But we were all like that proverbial frog that had been thrown into a pot of warm water, and unbeknownst to us, it was set to boil... We didn't know our asses were cooked until it was too late.

"By that time, we realized that the country had been stolen from us and Leftists were firmly in control of our culture, schooling, politics, and courts. They flooded our country with illegal aliens, essentially erasing our borders. They rewrote our language with their own version of Newspeak, so the constitution was effectively nullified or neutered. With these changes, they took away our rights to speak freely, possess firearms, practice our religions, assemble, vote fairly, and so much more. And yet while they did all of this, we did little to nothing. Most of us spoke out. But those voices were silenced, as you all remember."

Buford gazed over the bus and then back at Colin. No one dared to say a word.

"That was years ago." Buford looked back up.

"Many of us had not given up. But we knew we had to bide our time. We carefully built a group of fellow patriots who were willing to give up everything, maybe even sacrificing their lives to this cause of restoring our country back to its previous greatness. And today, we began a three-step process to take back our country..."

Buford looked like he was done, even though he'd only spoken in generalities, all of which his audience could have mostly stated themselves.

"Sir, could you answer the young man's question," Ben Shapiro asked and then snickered, "What is Operation Cow Fart?"

Buford let a smile creep up his face of wrinkles. "Of course. I was just about to get there."

Buford glanced up at the bus' ceiling, as if the words he were seeking were there, and continued. "We all see the ubiquitous Community Patrol Drones everywhere, either zipping by us or filming us or even worse, telling us what to do. But what many of you might not know, is these were the replacements to the local police forces around the country. The calls of racism and woke politics were too much for local politicians to handle. Every police force around the country was eventually defunded, disbanded and taken over by federal authorities. Of course, crime skyrocketed everywhere, especially in America's big cities. Leftists just didn't seem to understand that without law enforcement officers to enforce our laws, evil people felt free to commit crimes whenever they wanted. These drones were The Party's solution. They filmed and voice recorded law-breakers, and made announcements or threats to them. But they also did something else most of you don't know."

The bus hit a speed bump, jarring everyone, who had otherwise remained riveted in their seats, fixated on each of Buford's words.

"On every CP drone is an atomizer with various non-lethal compounds meant to turn away crowds with a noxious smell and even a gas to knock out those The Party deemed a threat. Then, ReAD Enforcers could come in and clean up. All we did, is use The Party's own drones on them."

Buford stopped and coughed twice. A couple of voices murmured "How?" as in *how did you do this?*

"Don't ask me the details of how we commandeered their drones. We have a lot of smart Patriots who want to see a different America.

"Chief among them was an Israeli scientist, who had found out that Leftism was physiologically similar to a disease. His research demonstrated that Leftism rendered its adherents—or infected, if you like—unable to question what The Party was telling them, while at the same time, completely incapable of understanding anything contrary. This is why it's so impossible to use logic to debate a Leftist."

Laura Ingraham, yelled out, "I told you it was a disease, Candace." The rest of the bus was a buzz with quiet mutterings, and most heads nodded up and down in agreement.

"Well, this same Israeli scientist also came up with a compound to neutralize the effects of this Leftism disease. And once this compound is introduced, it opens an infected's neural pathways again, enabling them to question what they're being told. Each person exposed to this formula becomes like a teenager who challenges everything his parents tell him.

"And one of our Patriots"—Buford tilted his head toward Colin and whispered, "It was your uncle, Noel"—"came up with the idea of spraying this compound on the Leftists in DC, under the guise of a fart cloud. The reasoning was that something as crazy as a toxic cow fart cloud would actually be believed by The Party, who would then use it for their own benefit, and CCPN would fan the stink of the crises all over so that the Party members would believe it."

Buford had spat out this last part of his speech in one hurried sentence.

"And continuing that thinking, by hitting the epicenter of American Leftism, specifically federal employees, lobbyists and politicians in DC all at once, we'd have a chance to shake up the country enough to change everything."

"Wait there, mister..." interrupted an ancient man with frizzy white hair and thick glasses, who stood up in the back of the bus.

"Please, you all can just call me Bob."

"Alright, Bob. You expect us to believe

that Leftism is a disease and that your secret scientist somehow developed a cure for this disease and you're spreading this cure, using The Party's own drones, in a gas form that smells like a cow fart? And, those Leftists, who were exposed, would start to abandon their religion of Leftism, questioning everything like a young mind typically does?"

"Yes, that's exactly what I'm telling you," Buford responded.

The man stared at Buford for a moment with utter bewilderment. Then his whole demeanor changed and he nodded. "Okay, I'll buy that. Thanks."

"Sir," Buford said. "What's your name and position, for everyone on the bus."

"You can just call me Bernie. I was a Senator and ran for President several times. I took some unpopular positions with The Party and they sent me here. Before today, I would have called myself a Communist... Now, I'm not so sure."

"And you accept what I'm saying, even as crazy as it sounds?"

"Yes, I'll buy it. It makes sense in a strange way. And now that you mention it, after what my new friend Ben Shapiro told me about Adam Smith's, Market Theory... For once, it is a lot more logical than the Communist-based or even Keynesian systems I believed in before. So, I guess cow farts are a good thing. In fact, I'd like to get back to asking more questions of my new friend, if you don't mind."

"Are you sure it's not aliens?" Nori asked.

"Yep, pretty sure."

Buford looked like he was going to sit down. But there was so much more to know, since he was being so open about the Patriot's plans.

"So what about the GPS?" Colin asked.

"That was us too," Buford said, in a much quieter tone. "We intended to disrupt just the GPS around the DC area, since only those employed by the Party or the super wealthy can afford cars anymore. We wanted to make sure they couldn't go anywhere. But I guess we got a little carried away and shut down the GPS systems around much of the US."

Colin scanned the bus to see if there were any other questions before he asked his last one, for now. "So what's next?"

"We go to a secret location where everyone gets off," Buford turned to Colin and lowered his voice, "then I'll take you back to your car, because you have some errands to run for your uncle, Noel." He projected his voice back to the end of the bus. "And then we wait for the magic to happen, after the drones have sent the cloud to Washington, DC.

Chapter 16
A little place in Mexico

Don Lemming continued to read the words The Party had given him. "It now appears that the cow fart cloud has picked up speed..."

Like it had a mind of its own, he thought.

"The OAS has now directed everyone within a one-hundred-mile radius of Washington, DC to return to their homes immediately. DC's Mayor has signed lock down orders, as the city braces for a direct hit from the toxic fart cloud, which has been said to have already killed millions."

Lemming had to forcibly restrain a laugh at this most recent assertion.

"Again, the Office of Approved Science has mandated all residents within a one-hundred-mile radius of the DC area to return home immediately."

His screen told him to take a break. On a separate display he could see, a new commercial from Big River beginning. He couldn't hear the audio, but he knew the ad: a popular face mask, which had been advertised before, with a few glaring changes: the price had been raised an additional grand to $1999 for a full-faced, cloth mask—*no profiteering there*; "Delivered by drone to your doorstep in one hour"; and the best change, a new banner proclaimed, "Certified to protect against toxic cow farts!"

Yeah, just like it did with COVID, Lemming's mind yelled out.

Before returning his attention to the tablets on his desk, Lemming gave a quick glance to the Picture Screen on the far wall, not surprised to see it had already changed again.

It was set to Default. On this setting, The Party used it to display everything from out-and-out propaganda to more obtuse Party-positive messages. The image usually changed about ten times a day.

The current image displayed a picture of their newly anointed president, AOC. This one showed her wearing a cloth mask, similar to the one just advertised, standing on the steps of the US Capitol, with a fist raised in the air. It reminded him of the old Nazi propaganda posters.

Regardless of its overt exploitation, any image was better than when the screen turned an eerie obsidian, which was meant to remind you that they were always watching you. But the worst was when the screen spoke directly to you. That had happened to him twice, and Lemming didn't want that experience repeated.

Lemming glanced back at his teleprompter to check on how much more time he had. Sometimes, like now, it listed a countdown clock to give him time for a bathroom break. It currently displayed, twenty-five seconds... Twenty-four.

He turned his attention to the screen of his black-market tablet, right next to a similar looking Party tablet, to research the actual cow fart cloud versus what The Party was having him report. He used his black-market tablet for anything that might be considered unacceptable to The Party, like reading unapproved stories or doing searches on illegal websites, like those supporting the Patriots.

In all of his research, through non-Party sources, he had yet to read even one report confirming a single death from the cow fart cloud. And yet The Party's narrative was that it had killed millions. His best guess was that there were two reasons for doing this. The primary one, was to stir up fear.

The Party's main mission was to create fear in its citizens so everyone would look to The Party for salvation. This mission of fear propagation had been at the heart and soul of The Party when it was just the Democratic Party, before the turn of the century.

Leftists later refined and perfected the wholesale proliferation of fear, through mouthpieces like him on 24/7 news channels.

Fear was the engine that drove every policy and every action of America's citizens: fear of guns, climate change, racists, viruses, unemployment, the other party, and so on. And when its citizens or corporations didn't bow down to that fear, or repeat its mantra religiously, they were canceled—at first socially and economically, and later, physically by brainwashing, literally, through reeducation camps. The other political party offered freedom, hope and prayers, whereas The Party offered fear. Fear always won.

The second reason for the Party talking up the severity of the fart cloud was a simple red herring. They needed to distract people, especially Party members, so they would ignore the installation of new listening and tracking software on Party members' tablets and Picture Screens. Lemming had witnessed this very thing happen to his own Party tablet. Unlike previous updates, where the user was first prompted to accept it before it updated the tablet, this one started automatically and then told the user not to touch the tablet while it was updating. Almost an hour later, his tablet was functional. And that was why they needed the diversion of the crisis:

to prevent members from using their tablets while The Party did its upgrade.

Of course, it wasn't like tracking and listening in on members was a new thing. For years he suspected The Party was tracking its members' speech and habits via their tablets, their RFID implants, and The Party's ubiquitous Picture Screens, all manufactured by the Chinese Communist Party in China. Seemingly simple actions like going to a Patriot-friendly website was considered seditious, which is why he had purchased a black market tablet to do his research. And just in case anyone might notice while he was on TV, this looked exactly like his Party tablet.

During breaks or interviews, Lemming would pretend to do work or type notes on his Party device, but he was really doing his own research on the black-market look-alike. There were two answers he was still seeking about the so-called fart cloud: where did it come from and was it toxic?

He could see The Party creating this fart cloud, then blaming it on The Patriots. He could see them even making it toxic, again to stir up fear. It wasn't like they really cared about their citizens. It was all about maintaining their power.

But something just didn't add up. Those exposed to the cloud were rendered unconscious, but to his knowledge no one had died. People seemed to react differently to exposure. The few reports he could dig up were almost immediately removed by The Party's own Reality Against Disinformation agency. The last report he was able to read, before it was erased, seemed to indicate that those exposed later awoke confused, with only a few feeling ill. Those exposed seemed to no longer obey Party authorities. This was huge.

If The Party created this, why not make it lethal and truly give people something to fear? And why would it cause those affected to be disobedient? It had to be the Patriots. The more he thought about it, the more he concluded this was part of a larger Patriot plan. He had read about the Patriots' plans to rise up against The Party. But every time there appeared to be an uprising in the making, it was quashed by The Party. They were just too strong and too controlling for the Patriots to make any headway. Until now.

Maybe they found a way through this fart cloud, he wondered.

His Picture Screen turned jet black, as if The Party had somehow employed Orwell's thought police so that they could read his seditious mind. He scowled at it, while gulping back bile. But then the screen changed to a new picture, this one of an AOC standing proudly in front of the newest American flag with 57 stars on it, and the message "One Party, Unified."

Lemming had a thought flash in his mind.

Now was the time to get out.

He had been planning to do this, but he had been waiting for the right time. In his gut he knew it was long past that time to leave town. Every day he waited was another chance for him to slip up and have The Party send him to a VETC. Plus, if the Patriots were truly making their move right now, he didn't want to risk it any longer. He may have been The Party's biggest mouthpiece, but he was expendable like everyone else in The Party. There was no reason to wait.

He had enough money spirited away in an untraceable account, all in a fake name, a fake RFID chip—that he would swap out for the one that The Party implanted in him, and a little place on the other side of the border... His little house on the coast in Baja, Mexico. With a little luck, they wouldn't even notice he was gone, until he was out of their clutches.

He decided at that moment, it would be tonight.

His ear-piece crackled and he looked up.

The light had turned green.

How long had it been?

Familiar music and then the spinning "Alert" logo, followed by the *Cow Fart Apocalypse* graphic appeared on the screen his TV audience saw.

I wonder what now? He thought.

But it wasn't anxiety at what The Party was going to do next. It was a feeling of serenity, one he had not felt in years. After tonight, he would no longer have to lie for The Party. He could take all the money he had made pimping himself all these years and disappear for good. Soon he would be sipping margaritas.

He grinned widely and calmly read. "The OAS has just handed down a new alert. The deadly cow fart cloud is expected to hit Wartington, DB—Good God, Bejing can't even spell our fifty-first state's name correctly"—*Oh shit, did I just say that? Just hold it together until tonight, Don* —"Sorry, that was Wash-ing-ton, D-C. The killer cloud of cow farts is going to hit the DC area at any moment. Return to your homes immediately."

Chapter 17
Let the fun begin

"It was an honor, Bob," Colin said, not even attempting to suppress the huge grin plastered to his face. He shook Buford's hand vigorously. "And thanks for the chance to meet all those amazing Conservative superstars." He kept pumping the man's hand without pause. "But most of all for telling me about Q. I still can't believe it's—"

"Don't forget what I said now. Mum's the word," Buford released himself from the younger man's vise grip.

Colin felt a tinge of embarrassment, but not wanting to be perceived as some silly fanboy, he bounded down the first two steps leading to the bus' front exit.

"Hey, don't forget this," Buford announced.

Colin saw Buford holding out his tablet. The one they had confiscated when he was arrested. The illegal one. Luckily, they had not removed his watch with his fake identity chip. "Damn. Yeah, thanks for that."

"And stay ready, Patriot," Buford said, releasing it to Colin with a reach. "Our next phase of Operation Cow Fart is coming soon and it's going to be even bigger than what we've already accomplished."

And what is that, exactly? Colin wanted to say.

"Sure wish you could give me more details." Colin looked up and searched the older man's eyes. They were a fortress, whose walls he could never breach, no matter how hard he tried. "I know, I know, it's for everyone's security."

Buford's mouth opened, about to release some tidbit of info, then snapped it shut.

A little crack in his wall?

"Just watch your tablet," Buford said. "I can tell you that you'll have a bigger role in what's coming."

Colin glanced again at his device, as if it had changed or would reveal something more than he was going to get out of Buford. He looked back up. "So what am I supposed to do until then?"

"Just continue doing what you've always been doing: go home, go to work, and do not act in a way that may alert The Party. At least not immediately."

Buford must have seen that he needed to offer him something more. Just a little, rather than leave Colin hanging like some unfinished series cliffhanger.

"It won't be long now, son. In fact, when you wake up tomorrow, it will be a new day, where most DC Leftists will see the world differently. Watch the after effects and enjoy." Buford now let a smile glide easily up his face.

Buford reached out for the button to open the door, but stopped. "Wait. Let's check our six and make sure there are no CP drones about."

Both of them scoured the sky outside of the bus' tinted windows until finally Buford was satisfied. He opened the door and released Colin.

Still, the moment Colin stepped outside, he felt like the eyes of the world were on him. With his feet planted on the pavement of the Moo Station parking lot, he allowed himself another glance at the sky. For a moment, he thought he had heard a drone-sound. Even though they had both just checked the sky mere seconds before and didn't see anything, drones were so quick and could appear at the snap of a finger. He did not want to have to explain to Party officials what he was doing getting off a VETC bus.

Right then, while searching for the non-existent drone, he thought up an alibi. He had fallen asleep in his car, after a long day at work. He woke to the sound of the bus driving up and he went to it to see if he could help. With the GPS systems all wonky, he thought a fellow Party member might need directions. Finally, after chatting with the driver, he got back off the bus.

I'd almost believe it, he told himself.

Bzzzzzz.

It was the startling but familiar sound of a CP drone buzzing overhead. It slowed to a hover right above him. And his alibi blew away in an instant.

He remembered he didn't have his Party RFID on him, which was still in his car. The drone would recognize him as a prole.

"Just be cool, Colin," he told himself under his breath. And just like that, his story changed. To support this, he did not wave back at Buford, who had pulled the VETC bus out of the parking lot and onto the road.

Colin was about to march over to his car, but abruptly stopped. He couldn't very well go to his Party car. Not yet. If the CP drone scanned him as a prole and then scanned him again at his car, it would pick up his Party RFID chip too. They would discover his ruse.

He decided to make his way into the Moo Station and wait it out there. As he started walking, one of Geely's newest models, a Green Utopia swerved into the parking lot at a high rate of speed. It zoomed alongside Colin, it's windows rolled down before it came to a stop.

Definitely a Party vehicle.

A man and woman were seated in its front seats, each pointing in different directions down the road, and then back at the restaurant. He could hear them arguing as he leaned closer to find out what they wanted.

The man spoke, "Excuse me," he said. A torrent of messed up hair fell over one eye, but he did not bother to move it out of the way. Colin noticed he had splotches of dirt all over his face like a common prole, but his fine androgynous suit was from one of the chic Party stores. The man's trap opened and then closed again, as if he were unsure what to say. Finally, he spoke. "We appear to have found ourselves without direction. We're trying to find our way home but our car will not tell us where to go. We ended up here although I cannot imagine why I would like anything made of soy."

"Wait," said the woman beside him, "JT, you said you loved my soy cooking. I think."

The man's head jerked toward the woman.

"Um, okay," Colin said, at first not sure if he should wait out their food argument, then deciding instead to help them get on their way. "Where's your home?" He examined the sky, no longer seeing the drone.

"Ahhhh," said the woman. "I know it's in DC in the Obama District. But I don't remember the address. Our car always took us there. Six-Six-Six-Something..." She trailed off looking up for reference. She looked as disheveled and confused as JT... *And the VETC guards.*

"This is a CCPN alert," blared their radio. "The toxic cow fart cloud is passing over Northern DC neighborhoods and will be directly over the Capitol and the White House in minutes. OAS has sa—"

The man punched the radio with a forefinger, silencing it. "Can you at least tell us how to get to that district from here?"

If the man could ignore that the so-called toxic cow fart cloud had found its way over or near their destination, Colin could too. He thought about their question. He did not know DC very well, but he knew where their district was located. He just wasn't sure how best to show them how to get there. Then he remembered he had a paper map in his coat pocket.

Buford had just given it to him, because it had the Patriot meeting point on it. He had already memorized its location, and was only holding onto it so he could ask Noel a question about this. He pulled the map out, opened it up and folded it into a neat square to show just their area.

"You are here," he pointed to a spot in the middle of the map square.

"What's this?" asked the man, looking more confused than before.

Perhaps they had never seen a physical map before, Colin wondered. "It's a map of the DC area. I folded it back to your area."

"But..." the woman cut in, "It's on... paper. I thought those were illegal."

Oops, he forgot about this. Probably not the best idea to wave around something that's been illegal for years. Paper was a luxury for Party members only, and a few Patriots who had stored supplies before the ban. Only days ago, his uncle showed him something called toilet paper, giving him a sense of a world where paper was so plentiful, it could be "flushed" away after cleaning yourself with it.

So that was a major mess up on his part.

"I know, right? I confiscated this at a prole's residence and figured a fellow Party member might benefit from it more. Especially with GPS acting all crazy now."

"Okay. I think I understand," said the man. "So, M... Muffy and I are here at this red "X", right?"

"No! I don't know what that is. *You* are here." Colin stabbed at a different place on the map. And you want to take this road"—he pointed at the map and then at the horizon, in the direction they needed to travel down the road—"all the way into DC. The Obama District is here. Maybe when you get closer, you'll remember your exact address. Or you could always look yourself up in your contacts, if you still can't remember." That last part seemed obvious, but as confused as these two were, he thought it might be helpful to remind them of this.

The man and woman just glared at Colin without commenting, like he had spoken to them in a foreign language.

The man turned away, just as Muffy said, "I want to go now, JT." JT apparently wanted to leave, too. He rolled up his window and sped away without so much as a 'thank you.'

"You're welcome!" Colin yelled. Party loyalists were often not very friendly. Though these two didn't seem to follow any Party norms, except for being rude.

Colin thought about Buford instructing the VETC guards how to shoot down the drones, and their following his instructions without question. Based on the behavior of these two Party members, Colin was convinced they too had been exposed to the fart cloud.

As he watched them speed away toward DC, he confirmed the drone was gone.

It was a good time to go.

But he held up and glanced toward DC.

He was too far away to really see it. But he could imagine a brown fart cloud covering the city and what would happen to the Party inhabitants after they were exposed to it.

Chapter 18
Bozo's end

Lemming turned to another camera to see Bozo, still in his bubble-boy suit, waiting for his introduction. He had almost forgotten about him. He was surprised to see the showboat was still in Washington, DC. Bozo obviously felt the suit would protect him or he'd have already made a run for it. The man was his own reality TV show.

"We return you to our man on the street, for perhaps his last broadcast... *Ever*"—*At least for me*, Lemming thought.—"Chris Bozo, what does it look like out there?"

"Don, as you have reported, the killer cow fart-cloud system is almost here," Bozo stated this in a voice sounding even more muffled by his suit than before.

The camera was focused first on Bozo's head, and then it zoomed past the White House, to the sky in the distance. There, a churning mass of dark brown clouds was moving toward them. The camera held onto this scene for a long number of moments.

"Okay, now focus on me, dude," Bozo whispered. The camera shuddered slightly and tilted down, refocusing on Bozo, from head to toe. With all the condensation inside Bozo's suit, it was almost impossible to see more than an ethereal image of Bozo in the fog of his own suit.

How appropriate, Lemming thought.

"Don, I stand here, with only a thin layer of protection, ready to face the cow fart cloud of death with no fear and no trepidation. And when it consumes me, I will not run." Bozo read mostly from his script, but added at the end, "...unlike all the pansy-assed, milk-toasts around here already have—"

"Chris, sorry to interrupt," Lemming cut in, and like Bozo, he didn't follow the teleprompter. However, in his case, it was because the teleprompter displayed both of their pre-programmed words, but it did not provide what his responses were to be when the showboat went off script, as he often did. But Lemming knew what The Party wanted to hear and he would speak their words...for now. "But the people have been given an order, direct from the OAS, to return to their homes."

"Riiiiight," Bozo stated, still continuing with his self-riotous, melodramatic, bloviations. "But none of them have put themselves here, with this great threat bearing down on them, like yours truly, ready to face their own mortality, without any fear and— Okay, what?" Bozo threw his arms up in the air.

"Hey," a trembling voice on the other side of the camera called out. A pointing finger shot out from the lower edge of the video. "You... have a tear in your suit."

"Whatyahmean?" Bozo asked, lurching his head down to inspect and then gesticulating his upper body to examine his back side, where the cameraman had been pointing. "Oh, my God!" Bozo screeched. He spun back around, while yanking at the material with his hands. A one-foot-long tear had opened, by the left side of his rear, but it got even bigger as he pulled at it. "Shit-shit-shit!" he bellowed.

Bozo glowered back at the sky. At the same time, the audience's view expanded to show a larger perspective of Bozo. Behind him was the White House and beyond that, the tip of the Washington Monument, already obscured by a swirling mat of brown.

"Help me get this fricking thing off, man," Bozo's voice rising to a soprano-like tone.

"Hell no. I'm outahhere," stated the cameramen. The video jostled and then dropped, until it came to rest hard on the ground.

The view was now of the black asphalt of Pennsylvania Avenue and a discarded face mask in the foreground. Bozo was bouncing around doing a convulsive-like dance in the middle-ground, as he pulled harder at the tear to force it open wider.

From behind the camera, a pair of man's legs appeared. They ran in front of the camera and then away from Bozo.

"Wait, where are you going? Get back here. I command you!"

"Chris, are you okay out there?" Lemming asked. The TV image still showed the pavement with Bozo hopping around while making the torn opening expand further upward.

Lemming wasn't sure what to do now because they usually cut away at this point. Beijing wasn't whispering in his earpiece, either. He continued to do what he assumed his TV audience would be doing. He just sat staring in bewilderment, as Bozo yanked and tugged at his suit in a frantic attempt to escape its captivity.

Finally, the tear was big enough that Bozo was able to pull his bare shoulders and head through. He wiggled his sweaty torso out of the opening, pausing to hyperventilate. Bozo's hands fumbled with the material in one last ditched attempt to unsuccessfully push it over his waist. He shuddered when he eyeballed the approaching cloud. Lemming figured that Bozo must have realized that the cloud would arrive before he could possibly free himself from his plastic bubble-boy suit. So, while still glaring at the fart cloud, Bozo bounded in the other direction, desperate to make a run for it. But his feet, now more constricted by the pushed-down material, barely moved. His top-heavy motion drove him forward, and Bozo toppled over toward the camera.

With his hands still tugging at his sides, Bozo crashed headfirst onto the asphalt.

"Oh, my God, Chris," Lemming blurted. "Are you okay?"

Bozo didn't move at first. Then he groaned. He lifted his head up slightly off the pavement, releasing a stream of red, which poured from his nose and forehead. His eyelids flapped open and the edge of his lip curled up, into a forced half smile, revealing a missing tooth and more blood. "I..." he said, in a voice that sounded under water.

His eyes focused on the old, discarded face mask in front of him. With great effort, one of his arms slowly scraped along the ground, until he was finally able to touch the edge of the mask. But that was as far as it went.

He lids flicked back closed and he let go of all muscle tension, sending his head back down to the ground with a sickening thud.

"Chris, can you still hear me?" Lemming begged.

Bozo didn't move.

A stiff wind blew in, whipping the trees in the background, and then Chris' mop of hair. The mask Bozo had so desperately reached for was swept away from the camera's view and then gone.

A darkness descended over the ground, as a layer of clouds blotted out the sun.

It has arrived.

The camera image went black.

Chapter 19

Get thee to the Bunker

AOC woke up in the dark, in a pool of her own drool. A dank smell assaulted her nose: a musty combination of puke and disinfectant. She had no idea where she was or even what day it was. "Hello?" She called out in a voice that didn't seem like her own.

A door burst open, sending in a blinding shaft of light that hit her aching eyes like a blast of cruel sunlight. She knew then that she was still drunk, so it hadn't been that long since she had passed out.

"I have the Snowflake-in-Chief!" someone announced, his body blocking some of the searing light.

A rush of people stomped in and headed right for her.

The lead of the group declared, "We're taking you to safety, Missy President." Two stiff arms hoisted her up onto her feet and carried her out the door.

This is sure easier than using my own legs to get around.

The hallway was chaos. People scurrying around in every direction, like field mice attempting to scamper away, all in a vain attempt to evade an unseen predator that they all knew was coming.

Now seeing them in the harsh light, she realized that the bubble of people who were surrounding and carrying her was her secret service detail. And *they* called her "Snowflake-in-Chief."

At that moment, she wasn't sure if that was meant as an insult or a compliment.

"Where we goin', Mr. Secret Service Guy?" AOC mumbled into the ear of the black-haired stud on her right.

"We're taking you to the bunker, Missy President. The toxic cow fart cloud has arrived. But we will protect you."

AOC had not been to the bunker yet, and had only heard about it. She gaped as they whisked her through crowds of workers she didn't even know. All parted like stream water around an unmovable bolder. They darted through the hallway and through a doorway. Its door snapped shut behind them. Dread filled her like the darkness of the stairwell they now raced down.

"What about all of those people..." AOC asked a little more loudly, so her words would be heard above the stomping of their feet on the metal stairs. "... You know, Mr. Sec-Service Guy... with the fart cloud?"

"Our priority is to protect you, Missy President. And my name is William Wood, but you can call me Will," he said effortlessly.

"Come on, hurry," urged HRC, at the bottom of the stairwell.

They banged their way down the flight of stairs, and through a hallway, barely lit by a few small lights. In the dimness, there was no definition or color to the people, the carpet, the ceiling, or anything. Though some of that may have been because of her own inebriated condition.

They slowed at a giant doorway that resembled a bank vault. Its metal door was swung open to accept those who were condemned to be locked up. She had a momentary feeling that she was going into a gas chamber, but she knew it was the other way around. The lethal gas was outside, already coming in.

"Let's set her down over there," Will commanded.

She was lowered to a cushy chair on wheels, similar to the one she had just been snatched from. Her Secret Security detail released her and motioned others in the hallway toward the door, which was already swinging closed.

AOC gave a frightened glance around the room and saw several dozen people. Besides HRC and a few high-end people in her administration, there were at least half a dozen Chinese ambassadors—she had more of these than Bill had interns—and still other people she'd never seen before.

She wondered if Bill was in here. But a quick check told her he wasn't

"Okay, we are good to seal up the room," said Will into the cuff of his gray jacket.

Several more of her detail slipped outside the door as it continued its slow swing inward. She wondered what they were doing outside, without the protections everyone in the room had. She was about to say something, when a husky female voice cried out, "Wait!"

It was a panicked HRC, who rushed toward the doorway, pushing passed one person after another to get there. *Was she going to find Bill?*

"Hold the door!" commanded Will.

He turned to HRC. "Ma'am, we can't let you outside. As the Chief of Staff, you must remain with the President." He stood in between her and the door that was open just a few inches now.

"But, I forgot my tablet," HRC begged.

AOC found her way to her feet and wobbled toward HRC, to offer some help.

"Missy P, you need to remain here," HRC stated. "I have to get my tablet. I left it on the Resolute Desk."

AOC knew this was her own desk in the Oval Office, to do the "President-stuff" she had to do. But HRC used it quite a bit to do her own work, often mumbling, "This should have been mine anyway" under her breath.

"Won't the tablet be fine when we return? I doubt it will be bothered by the cow farts," AOC said and guffawed at the mental image of HRC's tablet having a nose that wrinkled at the smell of a cow fart.

"I can't leave it, Missy P," HRC said, her brows furrowing like two canoes. "Because it has all my notes and emails, including all those I erased from my file server years ago." She leaned into AOC, "I don't want to make the same mistake Hunter did and have someone recover this if we're stuck down here too long."

AOC nodded but she wasn't sure if the Hunter that HRC was referring to was Old Joe's son, and now the new President of the Ukraine or someone different.

"Are you going to get Bill, too?" AOC asked.

HRC brayed her usual evil-sounding laugh, but stopped herself fairly quickly. "Hell no! He and his girly interns can suffocate in a plume of cow farts for all I care."

She pushed by Will. "Step aside, I need to get through."

"But we can't let you back in," Will instructed.

HRC stopped and briefly considered this. "Fine, after I retrieve my tablet, I'll go to the Situation Room. It has plenty of filters. I should be safe there."

"But you are not absolutely safe outside of this bunker," said Will.

That's when the severity of what was happening to them hit home. Even the studly leader of her Secret Service was afraid that this cow fart cloud could really kill. AOC found herself shrinking back into the safety of the bunker, away from the door. She desperately wanted it closed now, even if Hil was about to go out there and might not survive.

HRC slipped out the door.

"Close us in," ordered Will into his cuff.

The door closed with a deep thud that vibrated the floor beneath them.

A few people in their crowded group were crying. A few spoke in panicked voices. Others stared at the door that had closed them in for however long they were going to be there.

AOC just wanted to escape in sleep or play Candy Crush.

"Hey, Will. I'm not sure who to ask but could I get a Red Bull and a laptop computer?"

Will just glared at her, and disappeared into the next room.

That's when all of their lights went out.

Chapter 20

Big Brother is watching *you*!

"The Capital, the Pentagon, and the White House are now consumed by the toxic cow fart cloud," Don Lemming read.

He had just seen an alert on his black-market tablet that reported the White House had also lost power and communications, and no one knew why. He had to find out more.

He reached down to grab the tablet and accidently knocked it to the floor.

At the same time, he held his gaze at the camera flashing a faux smile. "That's the top story tonight."

As he waited for the booming music and graphics to subside and his teleprompter to tell him to start, he quickly snatched his device off the floor. He rapidly typed in the address to a Patriot website that reported on this kind of thing to see if there was any new information, while double-checking his teleprompter.

His device made a ping sound, and he glanced down to see a red banner across the search screen. "ReAD has deemed this site to be unsafe for viewing."

What?

Then he knew. His stomach was consumed in a torrent of fire.

I used the wrong damned device.

In his haste, he had grabbed his Party device to do the search rather than his black-market device. Now The Party knew he was doing an unlawful search. His job was to read the news that they gave him, not research it. This was an absolute no-no for Party members and would generate alerts to Beijing. It wouldn't be too long before the people above him realized it was him and did something about it.

He took a breath and glanced at the time. It was 7:52 PM. This wasn't an intractable problem. He would stop his broadcast at 8:00 PM, an hour earlier than he had planned. He would just walk away. They would buzz him and think he was just sick or something. They'd just program around him. And when they connected the dots, he'd be long gone.

Anxiety now gave way to excitement.

In only eight minutes, he would dash out of this life as a Party mouthpiece and start a new one, doing what he wanted to do. For a change. Eight minutes was an eternity for The Party. He might as well have some fun and get in a dig or two. But he had to be careful. If he said too much, they'd just pull his feed and his hundred-million-plus audience would miss his message.

Then, in the morning when they finally came for him, he'd be gone for good.

He caught a blinking green light and saw his teleprompter had once again started without him. His Picture Screen blinked and went blank and remained black, like it was dead to him.

His gut did cartwheels. *Could they have been that quick?* He tried to ignore it and continue.

"OAS is waiting for the cow fart cloud to clear before it can go in and assess casualties. They say that because all government officials have been given ample warning, they expect there will be few deaths at the Capitol or White House. Meanwhile they remain in communications with POTUS and other high-level cabinet officials..."

Now was the time.

"What I just read to you is not true. The Party is *not* in control of what's happening. I have read reports that the White House has lost power and communications. POTUS and her cabinet are still there. Is this part of a successful Patriot plot? And if so, that means The Party is definitely not in control.

For one moment, he once again felt like a real journalist. He had not felt this since his first gig on TV when he broke a story on corruption, all from his own research.

His earpiece crackled with angry Chinese. He looked at his TV screen to confirm he was still live. He nodded to The Party members in Beijing now paying attention to him and read from the teleprompter again.

"As you have already seen, we had lost contact with our correspondent"—he decided to add—"who had succumbed to his own stupidity and not a ludicrous cow fart cloud."

No stopping now. He would be gone in... four minutes. He might as well go out in style.

"The Party won't tell you, but this whole crisis was manufactured to make you afraid. Remember, if The Party can keep you afraid, they control you. Don't buy into it. Question everything you are told. Especially everything you hear and see on this channel.

"I have been lying to you for years. And here is my proof to you: after today, you will no longer see me on this channel again. I will be removed from the station because of my words against The Party.

"It's time you started thinking for yourself. Stop accepting what you hear or read. It's all made up by The Party. Come on, a killer cow fart cloud? Cows used to be eaten by us, not feared by us. That was until The Party outlawed them.

"Repeat, you have nothing to fe—"

Lemming saw that the camera light turned red just then. He also noticed that the television screen, which had been showing his broadcast live, was now showing commercials about an upcoming CCPN show, *How The Party Created a Green Utopia in America by Removing Cows.*

It was time to leave.

He yanked out his earpiece when his Picture Screen came alive with what he had hoped to avoid seeing.

It was Big Brother.

BHO, also known as POTUS 44, sat at a desk, wagging his long forefinger right at him. His short-cropped afro was as gray as volcanic ash. It made BHO look much older than he remembered. "Now-

now, Donny. I am not happy with you. But some of our people will be there shortly to speak with you. Don't do anything stupid. Wait right there."

Lemming burst from his chair and dashed out of the green room. Big Brother shouted out some other warning that he chose to ignore. He was a free man.

He was about to realize the biggest advantage to working out of his home, instead of the NYC studio the TV's portrayed: he could make his exit quickly and without being seen by others. He darted to a bedroom closet and from a back corner, he grabbed two thick bags. The one with his fake RFID, cash and gold coins was so heavy, he grunted to get its strap up and around his shoulder. The other, with a few changes of clothes, toiletries and snack bars was fairly light.

He found his way to his garage and set down his bags between the two parked vehicles. He focused on the one that was covered.

It was his fully restored Mustang, with an extra gas tank built in full of fuel. They sold fuel across the border, but he should have more than enough to get him through the border and to his place in Mexico.

He yanked off the cover, threw the bags into the front passenger seat and swung around the front to the driver's side.

In his hand, the car key was connected to a metal key chain he had from his college days, when he naively believed in its saying. It was a flowing flag with the monogram, "Freedom of the press!"

He chuckled at the whole sense of freedom as he started the car, relishing the sound. He thought that at least he would have freedom when all those other SOBs must continue to live under the Communist boot of The Party. All he had to do was get across the border.

He turned on his radio to the CCPN radio affiliate, to see if they mentioned anything about him.

He clicked on the garage door opener. The door responded with a grating stretch, as it slowly creaked open. He wouldn't have to worry about fixing this now.

Once more his stomach did somersaults.

In his driveway was a ReAD truck, and in front were six ReAD Enforcers with their weapons drawn.

"Hello, this is Brian Tater," announced a bald-headed man to the CCPN camera.

"I'm sitting in for Don Lemming, who is currently on indefinite leave. We'll all pray for his swift return.

"We continue our coverage of the cow fart apocalypse, which has crippled the nation and killed millions."

DAY TWO

Chapter 21
Is it January 6th again?

"They're coming to kill me!" AOC screamed, waking herself up from a reoccurring nightmare of the Capital Hill Insurrection of 2021. That day, as she had been told, there were millions of DJT's followers breaking down the doors of the Capital, with the intent of killing her and her Squadron members. Every night since, she woke from her nightmare, just as a scary guy, wearing horns, and yelling, "Make America Great Again," burst into her room.

"Are you all right, Missy President?" asked KH, who had been snoring in the seat next to hers.

AOC blinked at the single emergency light that seemed to blink back at her. In spite of this light and her irrational screaming, most in the room didn't stir. The glaring light cast a reddish gloom on the entire room which dimly reflected her own mood at the moment.

"Yeah, fine," she answered and shifted in her chair. She had been offered one of the other rooms in the large bunker complex, to "sleep off the alcohol," but preferred being in the big room with the others. Besides, her seat was comfy enough.

As difficult as it was to sleep, she was glad to have had enough rest to be rid of her drunkenness. The long cloud of alcohol was removed. What was left was a horrible post-tequila headache and an awful taste in her mouth like something had crawled in and died while she was unconscious. Worse was an overwhelming feeling of doom.

Somehow, even though they were supposedly in one of the safest and most impenetrable places on the planet, their power and communications were cut. To make matters worse, their tablets were disconnected in the bunker because, as she was told last night by one of her military peeps, the whole place had some sort of... *Friday cage around it?* She still didn't know what that meant, only that they couldn't connect with the outside world using any of their devices, whether calling out or checking their feeds from Twatter or Fakebook. All of this added to her building anxiety.

For as long as she could remember, she had never been disconnected from The Party. And she wasn't the only one: no one inside the bunker knew what was happening outside the bunker.

Is everyone dead? Is the cow fart cloud still there? Are the Patriots coming to kill her... again?

"Breath girlfriend," she told herself, trying to calm her nerves.

"I know, Missy P," said KH. "I was worried the cow farts got through somehow with the power not working the filters and what not."

"Duh, like we're still alive. So obviously..." she responded, tossing an unseen scowl at the woman, glad the lights weren't working at that moment.

She looked up as the emergency light blinked back at her once more. But this time, so did all of the other lights. Electronic equipment in the room and in other parts of the bunker beeped loudly, indicating they were waking up again. Her tablet buzzed and beeped, alerting her that she had many new messages, texts and emails.

Most of those in the room, like AOC, shielded their eyes from the sudden brightness.

Maybe darkness was better, she thought as her headache dialed up its severity several more notches.

A phone rang and a female Army general picked it up before it could ring again. "Right. Yes, she's fine," she said while scrutinizing AOC. "Yes. Okay. Thank you, Lieutenant." Female General placed the phone down in the cradle and commanded, "Please step away from the door. They're opening up right now."

On cue, the door issued an electronic hum and cracked open an inch. Those parked up against it stood up and scurried away. Half the room cheered.

"What did they say?" AOC asked the Army general.

"I'm supposed to escort you to the SitRoom for a debriefing," Female General told her and Will, who hovered nearby. "And the White House physician is waiting for you there, to examine you and make sure you're fine."

"Do you know why we lost power and communications?" AOC asked.

"You know as much as I do, Missy President." Female General replied.

With the giant door fully open, they walked out of the bunker. This time, AOC did it without being carried. But she couldn't shake the feeling that something else was off.

AOC didn't expect there would be many people in the perpetually dark hall and stairwell, connecting the bunker to the White House. But she did outside of this, in the main access hallway to the Oval and SitRoom, which was usually a buzz of activity. Now it was completely empty, except for them.

She wanted to ask her military escorts or Will, where everyone was? But a part of her didn't really want to know the truth. Just like all things with The Party, it always felt better to just assume they would take care of everything for you. But her knotted stomach told her she no longer felt this.

When they had arrived at the SitRoom, her doctor was already waiting for her. The room still had the musty puke-smell lingering inside.

AOC walked right up to him. "Hi doc," she said, while sticking out her tongue. "Ahhhh."

The doc scrunched up his face and twisted his head away from what must have been her breath. "Please, close mouth!" screeched the Chinese doctor.

"Sorry." She did, feeling a little embarrassed. She wondered if something did, in fact, die in her mouth. But before she could check, he stuck her arm with some sort of injection.

"Ow! What was that?"

"Anti-cow fart vaccine from our lab in Wuhan," he said with a counterfeit smile. He turned away and told Female General, "She cleared," and stomped out of the room.

AOC rubbed her arm, wondering how they could have created a vaccine in one day and shipped it from China, where all vaccines were made. How could they even know if a vaccination was needed, much less if it would work against cow farts?

She caught a glimpse of her soy candy bowl. It had been refreshed at the end of the table. She practically darted for them and her chair. "I'm soooo hungry," she said to no one in particular.

She planted herself in her chair and scooped up a large handful of candies into her trap. She was surprised to see that half of her cabinet members had already taken their seats. Female General closed the door behind her and was handed a tablet. She scrolled through and then nodded.

"Missy President," the general said. "I will be handling your debrief."

AOC shot a hand up in the air, but didn't wait to be asked. "Where is the other general who usually does that. You know, the sexy one?"

"General William Westmoreland III is currently in the WHMU," Female General explained. "That is the White House Medical Unit, where he is being treated for exposure to the cow fart cloud."

"Oh no, will he survive?" KH asked the same question AOC was going to ask, but she didn't hold up her hand. AOC tried to remember if holding up a hand was protocol. She couldn't remember, even though she had been through dozens of similar debriefs in this room.

"Yes," said Female General. "We expect him to make a full recovery."

"Where is the rest of my cabinet?" AOC asked, her hand thrust into the air and then immediately retracted.

"I don't have reports on all of them, but many are also at the WHMU," said Female General, "Because they didn't make it to the bunker in time."

"What about Hil? Is she okay?" She had started to raise her hand, but stopped herself. It felt like they were having a conversation and, therefore, she didn't need to ask for permission to speak.

"We don't yet know her location." The general looked back at her tablet. "So if I may continue... The fart cloud has dissipated. But it has left Washington in chaos. GPS systems are still mostly disabled and we're not sure—"

"—Umm..." AOC's hand blasted into the air again. "How many have died... You know, like from the cow farts?"

"I have no estimates, Missy President. But OAS tells us that they are not sure that the fart cloud killed anyone."

"Wait... What?" AOC looked at the others at her table, her hand still in the air. She was looking at their faces for confirmation that *this* fact seemed odd. Yesterday they were told that cow farts were deadly. "Okay, I guess it's just me, but haven't we been telling people how toxic this thing is? And didn't we make announcements that millions had died?"

"Then we were wrong, Missy President. We just didn't know when it was happening. And you don't have to raise your hand to speak."

AOC lowered it, feeling somewhat silly. "What do we know about the cow fart cloud?"

"Well, we know a lot. The cloud only hit north of DC and the greater DC area. Then it dissipated. We still don't know its origin. Everyone caught in the cloud, passed out, but only a few sustained injuries. Those injuries were not directly from the cloud, but from ancillary causes like passing out while driving their car or concussions from falls."

The general scrolled down her tablet, as if she were picking only the juiciest morsels of what The Party served her. "Because Party members appeared to suffer the greatest effects of the cloud, we believe that it was a Patriot plot to target Party members.

"Excuse me," KH asked. "If it was the Patriots, why did they send a toxic fart cloud that wasn't actually toxic?"

"We don't know the answer to that question," the general said, her eyes flitting around the room for any other comments.

"Do you have anything more?" someone asked.

"Yes, we have video of our operation to re-secure the GMU VETC. If you'll recall, the GMU VETC was attacked yesterday by the Patriots. When we had the 'all clear' today, we sent ReAD Enforcers back there to re-secure that location."

Female General pointed a controller at the screens and they came alive with more moving drone footage.

"Great, that's all I need," AOC quipped.

"Excuse me, Missy President?" the general asked.

"Nothing. Let's see it." AOC said, but she didn't look up. She hung her eyes on her own tablet, not just to avoid any feelings of nausea from each moving video, but because of something that drew her attention to her tablet's screen.

Only now had she finally glanced over her texts. There were many from various people she knew. But one stood out from last night.

HRC: "Got tablet. Not going to make it. Awful smell, like Bill's Macanudo cigars. I..."

Chapter 22
Have no fear, ReAD is here

A caravan of ReAD armored EV vehicles and two buses pulled up to the GMU VETC gate and stopped. Fred Serpico had been anxiously anticipating the armed convoy's arrival for hours. Now he waited for them to come to him.

One of their guards approached the caravan's lead vehicle, first glancing at the long line of vehicles, and then asking the driver for their copy of their Student Transfer Orders.

The guard didn't know it, but multiple weapons were aimed at his head by the ReAD Enforcers who were told to expect resistance. Serpico knew the procedures. He just wasn't sure how his newly aligned VETC guards would respond.

The VETC guard carefully compared the copy the driver just sent to his tablet, to make sure it matched the one sent to him by Washington. Next, he used his tablet to scan each of the occupants' RFID implants. Then he looked up from his tablet and gave a nod, saying "You and your party are authorized to enter."

The guard took a step back and made a motion with his free arm telling another guard to open the gate.

All weapons inside the vehicle were clicked back on safety. At least, that's what Serpico hoped.

The lead vehicle's driver tossed an odd glance at her commander in the passenger seat, as if to say, "Well that was easier than we'd thought, wasn't it?" The only reason they arrived with such a large force was because they were surely told to expect trouble. That the whole complex had been overrun by the Patriot terrorist group, who had released all the facility's political prisoners.

The driver radioed to the other vehicles in their caravan and tapped the EV's accelerator to quietly move through the gate. The other vehicles followed suit, along with two VETC buses in the back, each carrying a new load of students.

The VETC bus drivers had been ordered to hold back in the event of an armed conflict. That was also procedure. With the conflict removed, they were free to take their students directly to the processing center.

The lead ReAD truck passed through the entrance, and immediately its driver found what she had been looking for. A charging station. There, they found Serpico, a one-man welcoming committee.

The driver left room for two other vehicles to pull in and connect to the other two charging stations.

Serpico suspected all of the EV's were in a desperate need of a charge. But with more vehicles than charging stations, and the hours required to charge each vehicle's batteries, he knew they would have a problem. But he had other worries.

The driver exited the vehicle to hook it up.

"Hello, I'm Serpico. Do your people need any help?" Serpico asked the driver.

"Serpico, I'm the commander of this group," said a broad-chested man, stepping down from the vehicle's passenger seat. He held out his hand and shook Serpico's. "We were expecting to see trouble here. Where are the Patriot terrorists? And where are your wounded?"

Serpico restrained a smile, then answered soberly, "Thankfully, there were no serious injuries. All of my people were taken by surprise from the cow fart cloud. We were knocked out. When we came to, we found that the terrorists had taken our clothes, so they look like VETC guards. They stole a couple of

VETC buses and kidnapped our students. That was long ago. We reported all of this and we were expecting you hours ago. What took you so long to get here?"

The commander looked pissed at having to answer what seemed like a legitimate question. He huffed a heavy sigh and said, "Wasn't our doing. My team didn't get the orders until this morning. The Washington team that was supposed to be dispatched, couldn't be reached after they were hit by the terrorist's cow fart cloud. We're told that their entire unit succumbed to the toxic cloud."

"So naturally, Central chose your unit?" Serpico answered, wanting the commander to know he was following along.

"That's correct and our unit was three-hundred miles away. We responded immediately to our orders, which were to escort the two gas-powered VETC buses and to expect resistance."

"And of course, you were saddled with those EV's," Serpico added.

The commander gave a scowl, to let him know this was a sore subject, as it was with all the military who had to use a vehicle with maybe a hundred-mile range limit. "Your facility was way out of range for our vehicles, and we ran out of juice twice. What few charging stations exist out here were hard as hell to find with GPS still out. Anyway, we just need a charge and then we'll be on our way. With any luck, we'll be back home by late tonight.

"In that case, Commander," Serpico said, "I'll go help with the processing of the new students. We're a little shorthanded today."

"Of course. Thanks for making sure we have what we need. One Party United," the commander said raising a balled fist in the air.

Serpico didn't say anything in return. He just raised a balled fist for a moment, spun on his heels and jogged off toward the two buses, which had parked and were already offloading the new students for processing.

Serpico wasn't sure what he had expected, but Buford had told him it would be easy, no matter how many Enforcers showed up. He had been correct about everything so far.

Serpico had already prepped his VETC guards. Just as Buford had instructed, they were completely open to whatever he told them. In fact, they followed his requests to a "T." Buford explained that was one more benefit of the compound released in the fart cloud Those with a more Leftist way of thinking were more open to new requests. It was like a computer which had its programming erased and was now starting fresh, ready for new programming. So there was little resistance to any new suggestions he gave them.

This made sense to Serpico, who had been a long-time professor at GMU witnessing first hand as The Party indoctrinated young minds, already open to its early programming. He had been one of the few professors who had quietly resisted such efforts by teaching his students to think for themselves. Unfortunately for them, he was a lone voice in a sea of Leftist indoctrination, which rubber-stamped the kids into the radicals, who later became leaders of The Party.

But today was a new day.

Today, Patriots had reclaimed GMU from the Leftists, and as long as he drew breath, he would make sure their Leftist indoctrination would never take place here again.

As Serpico entered the gym, he could see that the new students had already been locked up in the holding area. ReAD Counselors were standing by, waiting to be relieved by VETC guards.

One of them, a nerdy fellow, with wire-rimmed glasses, hooked on the edge of his nose, looked up from his tablet and met Serpico a few feet from the holding area's fencing.

"The students have been secured," the nerdy guy said.

"Thank you. I will take over from here," said Serpico.

"Just you?"

"Yes, the rest of the incoming processing team are on break right now. We expected you hours ago."

"I know—I know. Not our fault. Okay, I'll leave you to it then."

The nerdy guy handed Serpico his tablet and Serpico signed with his finger and handed it back. "Safe return," Serpico offered.

The nerdy guy barely nodded and walked off with the other Counselors.

Serpico waited until they had left the building and he heard the buses start up their engines. Then he turned to address the newest of their so called students, locked up like prisoners.

Many of them looked scared, which was common when they first arrived. They had no idea what was ahead of them. The suffering for years as The Party's ReAD personnel worked to break each student down and reprogram them with The Party's way of brainwashing. Most eventually accepted it and were then released. Others resisted and were housed until they either accepted or went insane.

No more.

"Hello fellow Patriots," he said to the eyeballs fixed on him. "Have no fear, Patriots are now in control of this facility and you will be released soon. Be joyous because today is a new day for America.

Chapter 23
The Naked Party

As Colin pulled into his parking space at Abound Energy, he could not shake the feeling that ReAD Enforcers would be there waiting for him. But everything looked normal.

"Good morning, CB," the receptionist said with her usual welcoming smile, "NF asked you to see him when you came in. He's in the B facility now."

"Good morning BC... Okay, thanks," Colin replied, sure that the Enforcers would be waiting for him on the other side of the public area. But after he left reception, he was not molested by anyone.

Colin made his way to the "B" or Bovine Facility, via the break room, excited to debrief with his uncle. But he just couldn't push aside his building anxiety. It was true, he should have been jubilant as his uncle and Buford and other Patriots had achieved some measure of success, not the least of which included securing his freedom. But the successes did not seem big enough to warrant celebration. And this is what fueled his worry.

At his locker, he changed from his classic suit and tie into the jumpsuit he wore for work. He stowed away his Party tablet and watch, and put on his Patriot watch with its false RFID. He pulled out his illegal tablet and pressed his thumb on the screen to turn it on.

It had been properly stored in a lead-protected sleeve in his suitcase on the way to work, as he was being uber careful to avoid any mistakes which might alert the Party. But now he was anxious to see if he had any messages from Buford or Noel, preparing him for the inevitable let down that was about to come. He felt sure he would receive some sort of negative news or see the red Party warning splashed across his screen, informing him that The Party knew what he did and to stay where he was as someone was coming to get him.

Of course, there was no such message. In fact, there was nothing to indicate that the Patriots were failing. Though there wasn't a lot of evidence that they were succeeding. Nothing either way. And nothing was almost worse than the imminent Enforcers kicking in your door, bursting in and taking you away. The public news was no help either. Quite the opposite.

From the time he had arrived at home, until leaving this morning for work, there was nothing really that inspired him to believe that today was that "new day" Buford had told him it would be. This is what fueled his doubts that all of their efforts had not worked and that The Party would connect the dots, learn of his secret identity, and would come for him. Then, all of the hope that had swelled up in him after the past twenty-four hours, would be smashed to bits.

But every moment he was free and didn't see Party officials busting down doors, offered just a little more hope that things would somehow be different.

He found himself practically sprinting from his locker into the breakroom.

Noel was there, casually sipping on a cup of Joe and watching the news from one of the tables. He turned his head and smiled at Colin. "Welcome home, Colin. Glad to see you were not hurt."

"Where were you?" Colin practically demanded. "You arranged for me to meet you, right when ReAD Enforcers stormed in and took us captive. I've been shitting bricks ever since."

Noel radiated his usual unworried demeanor, his warm smile still there. He ushered Colin to sit beside him. It was his here-comes-a-teaching-moment speech that Colin had been given more times than he could count.

As jittery as Colin felt, the last thing he wanted to do was sit down. But this was how his uncle rolled. So he forced himself to be calm.

"Sit, son. And let's talk," he said and waited for Colin to take a seat.

He leaned forward. "What you didn't know was that everything was happening so quickly, and I had to proactively implement potential damage control with The Party. But it was all to make sure that they believed in our cover story while Operation Cow Fart proceeded as planned."

Noel gingerly took a sip from his cup, his smile unobscured by the steam coming from the hot liquid.

"I had intended to meet you for a burger and then go home, *before* setting that part of our plan into action. But everything came together quicker than we had anticipated. Plus, I knew Buford would protect you and fill you in on some of the details of our plan."

His uncle sat back in his chair and grinned, knowing that his words were having the intended calming effect on his nephew's nerves.

"Okay, I get that. Buford explained a little of what the plan was, as farfetched as it seemed. But nothing has really happened." Colin shrugged his shoulders. "I was expecting a revolution with guns and bullets and fighting in the streets. But there is none of that. So many Patriots have said the only way we could take back our country is by force."

Noel listened patiently. When Colin had finished, he took a healthy gulp of his coffee. "We still don't believe it will be necessary to reach that extreme. We never wanted Americans fighting Americans. We did that once over the vile practice of slavery and State's rights, with brother pitted against brother. Millions perished and the nation nearly destroyed itself in the process. We never wanted to do that again."

"But in a sense, we are all still slaves to The Party. Why not a revolution, if that's what it takes?"

"For several reasons, son," Noel said in his Morgan Freeman professorial voice. "Most Americans do not have the stomach for fighting a war, American killing American. We would then lose a large segment of the country, already susceptible to Party influences, who would turn against us when blood was shed.

"Then you have to worry about Beijing. We've been dependent upon China for everything for so long. The Party has been so intertwined with them that a bloody war would only encourage them to send in additional troops to supplement the troops they'd long since integrated into our military.

"No, we had to approach this a different way. To change the hearts and minds of those in power, here in America. We knew The Party was top heavy. All we had to do was change a few people at the top. But replacing them wasn't an option. We already know that all elections are scripted and corrupted to elect Party members only. We had to change the minds of those at the top."

"Ergo, Operation Cow Fart," Colin said.

"Yep, Operation Cow Fart," Noel repeated.

"But the news reports said that many of the elite Party members and much of the government shipped out of DC before the cloud hit. So how could it have been enough?"

Buford's grin grew, as if he knew Colin would say this. "Have you ever heard of the parable: *The Emperor Has No Clothes*?"

Colin shook his head.

"An emperor, who loved fine clothes, unknowingly hired swindlers to weave him the best clothes in the land. Instead, the swindlers pretended to make them out of thread so fine, they were hard to see. In fact, there was nothing there. Yet, everyone in the emperor's kingdom was too afraid to let on that there was nothing there. Even when the emperor paraded around without wearing a thread, all said his clothes were the finest. Except a little boy, who told the truth, saying the emperor was naked. That was all it took: one little boy. One by one, their people snapped out of their group-think and spoke out, stating that the emperor had no clothes on."

Colin had a look that went from understanding to confusion.

"The point is, all we need are a few people to recognize that Leftist thinking is naked."

Colin's pensive face told Noel he was seriously considering it. Finally, he nodded and said, "Fine, but what's next?"

"We wait for our work to take effect. That's when enough of the population will come to realize The Party is not wearing any clothes."

Colin huffed a sigh. "Minus the clothes analogy, that's what Buford said... But I'm tired of waiting."

Noel's smile opened up into a chasm. "Patience, my boy. This has been in the planning stages for many years. It's only the start of what's to come. You'll have a larger role in the next phase."

"That's also what Buford said."

"Smart man. Maybe you should listen to him, too." Noel took another gulp from his coffee cup.

"Okay, fine," Colin said, not trying to hide his frustration. "But, other than a few confused guards at one VETC, I don't see any proof that this thing amounted to much of anything."

"That's because you're not watching for signs of change, of which there are many. Trust in the plan, son. Be patient. Watch carefully and you will see the signs." Noel stuck a forefinger up and turned up the volume of the television. "For instance..."

The CCPN broadcaster, a bald guy this time, was talking about how a small regional election in Georgia, had gone to a Patriot member, even though The Party candidate was expected to get at least 90% of the vote. "OAS believes this must be the work of the Patriots, who had an insider at Domination Voter Schemes. Meanwhile, Domination's CEO has succumbed to injuries sustained by the cow fart cloud."

"See, it's already happening," Noel said, sitting back in his chair, grinning from ear to ear.

Chapter 24
Can we lie enough?

"It appears that the cow fart cloud that blew in late yesterday, after killing millions of citizens, has now been dispersed by the government. This per an OAS alert."

The reporter's bald head glistened like a white cue ball about to be whacked by the pool cue. "This is Brian Tater, from CCPN Headquarters in New York City. As we continue our reporting on the Cow Fart Apocalypse."

The theme music they had been using for over 24 hours drowned out all other sounds, as the twirling graphic that tens of millions of viewers had become familiar with, spun around and then exploded on the screen. Finally, the special theme music ebbed and CCPN's regular theme music resounded. Then it too ebbed.

"All morning, we've been receiving reports of catastrophic damage caused by the cow fart cloud, which has since disappeared because of the masterful work by OAS engineers. We now have an update.

"Just moments ago, we told you that the CEO of Domination Voting Systems, which controls voting in all 57 US states, has succumbed to the fart cloud. Further, Patriot terrorists have used this crisis to steal one local election. We now go to Ashley Jiang, our reporter in the field in Virginia to bring you more on this story."

Tater turned to his right but didn't see the green light, or his teleprompter's text, or the video images that this adoring TV audience would be seeing. He heard Ashley sigh into his earpiece, but he couldn't see her. Then, someone started typing a message on his teleprompter screen...

HEY TATER, YOUR OTHER LEFT

Tater read the text letter-by-letter and then realization hit him like an electric shock. He spun his chair to his left. He stopped partway and did an over-spin to his right, rotating a full one-eighty until he was facing another bank of screens, where Ashley's image was waiting for him.

"Oh, there you are, Ashley. Wow, you're looking mighty nice today."

"Shut up you turtle—Wait, I'm on?—Hello, Brian." Ashley straightened her transparent miniskirt, looking down to make sure she was wearing the right undergarment, this time. Satisfied, she tilted her head up and let her face erupt into a grin. Then remembering this was supposed to be a more somber moment, she let her newly botoxed lower lip drop.

"I'm in front of the palatial home of Bud Mammon, the beloved CEO of Domination Voting Schemes, who was caught in the fart cloud while dinning at La Tête De Merde, the famous DC Party restaurant.

We've confirmed through security camera footage that the restaurant was consumed by the toxic fart cloud, causing all patrons to cough and gag. Mr. Mammon, who dines there regularly, passed out. One of his female companions, perished by drowning in her bouillabaisse. When an OAS team could reach him, he was flown by medical helicopter to his home, where his private doctors have treated him and said he should make a full recovery."

A man stepped in front of Ashley and yelled, "Patriots rule, man! The Party sucks!" Then the man ran off. Ashley turned in his direction, holding up her middle finger. She threw her offending hand behind her back, smiled and turned back to the camera.

"Ah sorry, Brian. Back to you."

Brian looked to his right and then back. "Ah thank you, Ashley." Brian turned his chair to his right.

"We break in our regular coverage to give you this alert."

Tater paused as the flashy "Alert" logo appeared on the screen, along with a loud beeping tone. This represented the queue for the audience that a brand-new alert was about to be handed down from their news desk in Beijing. And he was to bring this alert to them before anyone else, because they were the exclusive news network out of Beijing. Alerts were often very exciting for him, because he felt so privileged to be trusted by The Party to read these alerts. He began to read and then gulped back his breath, terrified at what he was reading.

"Sources have informed us of witnesses reporting a new cow fart cloud spotted east of Los Angeles and moving West toward the greater Los Angeles area. We're waiting for confirmation from the OAS, which has stated that because of the stink from that area, it's too hard to tell if it's cow flatulence or just the normal brown haze of the LA area.

"I repeat, a cow flatulence cloud has been reported just east of LA and is moving toward the city. Stay tuned for continuing coverage of the Cow Fart Apocalypse."

"I'll die before I surrender," Don Lemming hollered out the window.

He revved his engine over and over again. He was attempting to intimidate the border guards, who had probably never before seen or heard a gasoline engine with so much horsepower. But in reality, he was eyeballing the best place to break through the barrier erected to keep him from crossing the US/Mexico border.

All day he had been evading ReAD Enforcers. First at his Los Angeles home, when he punched through the Enforcers, scattering them like pigeons fluttering away from his death mobile. He was miles away before they caught up with him.

Then he lost them in traffic, because their vehicles were too big and clumsy to zig-zag around other vehicles. Then he lost them again when they ran out of power, because their vehicles barely made it one hundred miles before a charge.

But another group of Enforcers caught up with him and he gunned it for the border. Once there, he thought he had made it. Then he saw the barricade on the US side, erected to stop him. It was as if The Party had similar dealings with Americans trying to escape their totalitarian rule.

But he wasn't giving up. He'd invested too much time and planned this for too long. If he could only find one opening.

At last, he saw his opportunity and released his brake, while stomping down on the accelerator. The tires responded immediately, spinning in place for a military-second. It felt glorious. He was off.

He rocketed straight for the largest cluster of vehicles and ReAD Enforcers blocking his way. At the last second, he did something they didn't expect.

He spun the wheel and darted to his left, into oncoming traffic.

He knew that the border was heavily patrolled when leaving the US, because they didn't want anyone to leave. But coming into the US, no problem. They let anyone cross the border ever since The Party took over total control and installed their Puppet In Chief in 2020.

Other than a trickle of vehicles coming toward him, he had nothing to stop him now.

Just one hundred yards separated him from freedom. If only he could cross without hurting his vehicle or himself.

He swerved from one lane to the other, narrowly missing each vehicle slowing down when they saw the crazy vehicle headed their way. Although he was getting honked at by each vehicle he passed, there was nothing else obstructing his way to freedom.

Seventy-five feet to go.

He could already picture himself on the back porch of his humble twenty-five-thousand-square-foot bungalow, sipping umbrella drinks, served to him by his own servants while entertaining his neighbors. Perhaps one of the movie starlets or even Suckenberg himself would come over.

Just fifty feet more to g—

Dozens of CP Drones appeared out of nowhere, hovering a few feet off the ground, directly in front of him. Just before he passed through them, a vapor came out of each. He imagined The Party thinking of him, as a bug and they were spraying insecticide–even after all his years of service. He would squash them first.

He gunned it through the mist as the CP Drones drifted higher and out of his path, like flies when a swatter is pulled out.

As he passed through, he held his breath thinking he could avoid the effects of whatever they sprayed at him if he didn't breathe it in.

But he felt the effects instantly.

Barely twenty feet from the border, after swerving around the final car in his path, the world around him swam. Like the warm ocean he would never enjoy.

He blinked back the misty sting and saw the eyes—bigger than two Sonoran suns—of a Mexican border guard glaring back at him. The man ducked behind a gate post just as Lemming crashed into it, going fifty miles per hour.

Chapter 25

You're fired!

"I demand to know what's happened to HRC, right now!" AOC said while standing and waving her tablet in the air.

This was the third time she had made this demand. Each time, Female General told her to calm down. They would locate her and she was sure to be fine. That was when AOC lost her temper. And this time it wasn't an act. She was really angry. She was about to run from the room and search for HRC herself.

A phone rang and KH, being closest, picked it up.

"It's her!" she yelled jubilantly.

"Hil, thank mother earth you're alive!" KH's face went from euphoric, to shocked, to serious. "Okay... Yes, I'll tell her. Of course, I w—. Hey, you don't have to be so mean." KH put down the phone and sat back hard in her chair. The room was silent.

"*Well?*" AOC thrust both hands in the air.

"Oh sorry," said KH. "That was Hil—I mean, HRC."

"We got that. What did she say?" AOC leaned forward in her chair, both frustrated and not wanting to miss a word.

"Well, she sounded strange at first."

"How?"

"Oh, I don't know. She was just... different."

"I swear I'm going to slap you if you don't tell me exactly what she said." AOC wanted to do more than that at this point and couldn't understand why her ReAD Czar was being so obtuse.

"Fine. She first said, 'Shut up bitch!' That's what got me because she's always so nice to me, but this was bordering on hate speech—"

"Continue, for God's sake."

"Okay, then she said that she was fine and that she is 'now in the Oval, preparing your speech to the country.' When I told her that I would tell you, she got real mean and told me to, 'Not screw this up, like you did everything else, you stupid whore!' KH sat back in her chair again, fighting off tears that had welled up in her eyes. It was obvious that she was in need of a safe space. AOC couldn't help but also think this was odd coming from HRC.

She may have been as fake as a stack of $3000 bills, but you could always depend on her going the Party way. And The Party wrote her speeches, not HRC. *Why the changes?* She wondered.

"Was that it?" AOC asked.

"Just..." KH blotted her eyes with a tissue. "... Just that when you're done here, go and see her in the Oval." KH started sobbing again.

"We're almost done, Missy President," said Female General, who scrolled down her tablet before she resumed speaking. "We have reports of several officials of The Party who are under medical care after being exposed. They've experienced some peculiar... changes. Bud Mammon, CEO of Domination Voting Schemes, has been babbling about changing the voting software to count both sides fairly. Jeff Bizarro, the owner of the Washington Compost and Big River, was in town and this morning his paper printed some unflattering things about you, Missy President."

"Wait, that doesn't make any sense. They love me." AOC said.

"Hold on," KH says, looking at her own tablet. "Can you turn on the news, general?"

Female General used her device and turned on the news, but it looked different than CCPN. It reminded her of the old Fox News days, when a few of the news channels actually reported stories which were not supportive of The Party.

"I'm sorry, Missy President. This is supposed to be the CCPN Channel."

Only the logo on this news channel said, "The Patriot Channel."

"But how can this be? This is the terrorist organization and their false news feed, Right?"

No one said anything. They just watched in horror as the reporter told of a protest forming in front of the White House.

The news camera showed hundreds of people with signs that said treasonous things like "Cow Farce" and "Impeach AOC."

It was too much for her to take.

AOC stood up with such force the chair she was sitting in flew away and banged into the wall with a *thunk*. "Something is wrong," she announced. "I don't believe this. I have to go see HRC. She'll straighten this out. She always makes things right."

AOC dashed out the door and ran for the Oval office, a few stuttering steps away.

It was like she woke up in a scary version of The Twilight Zone or some alternate universe. There had to be an explanation for all of this. She knew HRC would figure it out and tell her what to do, just like she always did.

One of AOC's Secret Service team raced ahead of her and pulled open the Oval Office's western door. She entered and abruptly stopped.

HRC was sitting at the Resolute Desk. She stood up, glared faint recognition at AOC, and beckoned her to come forward with a hand.

But everything was wrong with HRC.

Although she was still old, she was now wearing a dress, not the same pantsuit outfit she'd been wearing for years. She looked... *tasteful*.

"Madame President," HRC said, not at all following the salutations AOC had requested upon taking office. "Please come here and sit beside me. We need to talk."

AOC felt like she was in a new nightmare as she sat in the offered chair, beside what should have been her own chair.

HRC told her what had happened. She awakened from the gas and quickly felt like a confusing fog had lifted. She turned on a TV and that's when she had made some decisions.

She kicked Bill out of the White House this morning, dressed and started writing the President's Address to the Nation. It was simple, AOC would resign and others would step in to take over and enact tax cuts; welfare reform; enforcement of immigration laws, including kicking out illegal aliens; disbanding several federal agencies... She continued for several minutes, running through a long list of mostly Conservative policies.

AOC's head was swimming.

"Here's your speech. You'll record it in the Green Room. You can go now."

"HRC, what happened to you?"

"I guess you can say, I woke up and finally saw the light. And my name is, Hill—"

There was a horrific noise on the other side of the Oval Office, causing both women to turn their heads and rise from their seats.

It was the Picture Screen, which normally showed pretty pictures and sometimes moving pictures of AOC and other Party members. This time it showed Big Brother.

His entire face occupied the width of the screen, and by the looks of him, he was pissed.

"I am so disappointed in you, Hill—"

"You big blowhard. You already know what I think about your disappointment."

She thrust her two middle fingers in the air.

AOC didn't know if she should laugh or puke at HRC's defiance.

"Now-now-now, that's not acceptable," said Big Brother. "We need to—" The screen changed again and this time it was blank, but not black. AOC had never seen the screen do this.

Then words started to scroll...

WE ARE TAKING BACK OUR COUNTRY!

More coming soon.

Q.

Chapter 26

We return you to your new normal

John and Muffy Tipton finally arrived home completely changed. They just didn't understand how... yet.

After driving around the city, they followed that Party member's advice at Moo Station, looking up their address when they reached their district.

"I can't wait for my soy espresso," declared John as he approached the door. "Wait, that sounds disgusting."

He waved his wrist and their front door opened.

"At least something is as we remembered," Muffy said, as she pushed through.

John's tablet pinged and he saw he'd just received the morning edition of the Washington Compost. He vaguely remembered enjoying this every morning. He stepped through the door, closing it behind them, hoping to experience some normalcy inside their home.

They both made their way to the bedroom, lumbering up the stairs. They were exhausted after experiencing the fart cloud, waking up disheveled and confused, getting lost in the country, and then driving around the city all night. As much as sleep would be welcomed, they wanted to watch the news. They were dying to find out what had happened to them, to the rest of the city and why.

John sat at the end of his bed and tapped on his tablet to examine the Compost while Muffy pulled out her own tablet to turn on the television and find some news.

John screwed his eyes at the headline on the front page: "Cow Farce Cloud?" *Should it not have said, "Cow Fart Cloud"? Were they making a joke?* He wondered.

He giggled at the political cartoon below this, depicting their female President ducking into the White House, just as a billowing brown cloud approached. She was yelling, "Help! Cow Farts!"

"I can't remember exactly. But I don't think we like her, do. we?" John said.

Muffy was trying to recall how her tablet worked with the television.

"Did you try the "On" button," John suggested.

Muffy glared at him and pressed the representation of an "On" button on her tablet. The TV turned on, just as he had suggested.

It flashed a warning that a new download had occurred and it was safe to begin viewing. Muffy selected the *News from Yesterday* channel, which displayed the news from the previous 24 hours.

John, in an attempt to get comfortable, tossed off his high heels and grunted at the pain. "Why do people wear these things anyway?"

"I don't know why men would wear them. They exist to make women's legs look longer and sexier," Muffy stated. She looked puzzled as if what she said wasn't what she planned to say.

John stared at her and could only say, "Oh."

The TV began showing yesterday's broadcast of President AOC at an official book burning ceremony.

The President struck a match and it roared to life. She tossed it into a pile of books, arranged on the ground. Beside the President were several pasty-faced people, each of whom tried to look more dower than the other. The books flamed up, but no one, including the President, moved away from what should have been a very hot fire.

"Why are they burning books?" Muffy asked.

"They're really not burning them. It's all fakery," John explained. He pushed his mop of dirty hair back to one side of his head. He couldn't understand why he let it get this long.

Muffy got up from the bed, went into their closet and fished around for something. She came back out a few seconds later. "Okay then, why are they pretending to burn books?" she asked.

"Because they believe the content of those books might be harmful. I guess."

"But no one is being forced to read them, right?"

"Now I know," John said poking his forefinger at the screen. His mop of hair fell over his eyes once again. "I definitely don't like her... Or The Party."

Muffy put something on his head, tucked his errant hair underneath and snugged it down further. "There, that's better," she said.

"What it is?"

"A baseball cap you used to wear," she said. "For some reason, it seemed appropriate now."

John stood up and walked over to their Picture Screen, which was set to Mirror, and examined himself in it.

It was a red baseball cap with lettering on it.

"Hey, what does MAGA stand for?"

Epilogue

Lemming woke from a very pleasant dream. He was in a lounge chair on the expansive patio of his beach bungalow. He was being fanned by bikini-clad young ladies while drinking umbrella drinks, one in each hand. He turned to the girl on his right, who was speaking Chinese to him. Then he turned to the one on his left, to ask what the first one said. He thought this one looked an awful lot like their currently anointed President. To his knowledge, he'd never seen her in a bikini. Then an image appeared, like a ghost, which materialized before him. It was Big Brother and he was wagging his finger at Lemming. "I told you that we would get you."

Lemming was jarred awake, blinking his eyes, trying to make sense of what he was seeing and where he was.

He was on a stretcher, being carried by two men. He didn't feel any pain, though he remembered being in an accident.

He lifted his head and saw his destination.

Panic took over and he thrashed about wildly. But he was too restrained and his movements barely registered to his handlers.

His hands and legs felt glued to the stretcher, so only his head and neck could move. "Stop!" He tied to yell at them, but it came out as a muffled, "Sto"

His handlers only paused their conversation for a moment, without slowing their speed.

"So, this one's not going to our facility in LA because that cow fart cloud hit it?

"Hey, you know as much as I know at this point."

"I guess that's why we're using the old VETC bus, then?"

The other didn't answer, but the words pierced Lemming like a hot poker: VETC bus. That meant he was going to a VETC reeducation facility.

"I guess this guy is going to be in good company," said the handler in front.

"True. I hear Fakebook's CEO is there too," said the handler behind him. "And the former governor..."

"Blather Newsom," replied the Front Handler.

"Right-right. I hear they were all trying to get out of the country and The Party didn't like it," replied Back Handler.

"I don't feel bad. Not like we're insiders in The Party."

"I hear The Party is falling apart anyway, because of this whole Cow Fart thing."

The two handlers started to hum the dreaded CCPN theme music of the Cow Fart Apocalypse.

It was at this moment Lemming knew he had to be in hell.

Tell Others...
"Cow Farts Apocalypse **Doesn't Stink!"**

We can be sure that a large number of Leftists will berate this book with their hateful words.

So it is up to you.

If you enjoyed any of this, please rate this book and write a quick review on the platform you purchased it from. Also, please rate and write a few words on Goodreads.

Then, ask your library to stock a copy; request your neighborhood bookstore to carry one or two; tell your schools to teach on this subject; and buy extra copies for your friends who need to better visualize what an unfettered Leftist takeover of America could look like in a few years.

Thank you!

EMC

1984 is Today

If you've noticed similarities to George Orwell's seminal work, *1984*, you would be correct. *Cow Fart Apocalypse* is meant to be a more contemporary version of the warning heralded by Orwell in his book, *1984*, except in parody to make it a more fun read. The similarities to Orwell's version of the future are purposeful.

1984 was published in 1951, and decades later, its terminology has been integrated into today's culture: Big Brother, thought police, Newspeak, and so on. Orwell's idea of the consolidation of societies into three separate totalitarian mega-powers: US & UK (Oceana), Russia & Europe (Eurasia) & China (Eastasia) is not far-fetched. Ask yourself, who are the superpowers today?

Orwell's book was a warning to all of us to watch out for the doom that our society would suffer under the heavy foot of Communism. And yet today, generations later, it would seem that this message was lost to a large segment of society. How else could you explain that so many children and young adults believe Communism, or at least Socialism, is a good idea, which hasn't been really explored yet. Likewise, that capitalistic societies are evil?

It was for this reason that I decided to take up the mantle from Mr. Orwell and shine the light on contemporary politicians who have spread the belief that we should give Democratic Socialism a try here in America. This book is an envisioning of what that world might look like. Even though it's a fictional parody, it's hard not to see the possibilities of the disease of Leftism taking root and infecting enough of us so as to destroy our future... That is unless we stop it now.

It is up to each of us to spread the word. Discuss books like this one and most especially Orwell's. Be involved in vigorous debates with those you disagree with. Articulate why the God-given freedoms we hold so dearly are the cornerstones to a vibrant and free society. Whereas, totalitarian governments, no matter what they are called, which control its peoples' lives, have been and always will be the true evil.

Thanks for reading and spreading the word!
E.M. Cooter

A little about *EM Cooter!*

E.M. Cooter is the pen name of an international best-selling author. She represents the typical American who is fed up with the anti-American views of Leftist politicians who spend wildly on pet projects and continue to take away our citizen's God-given rights as enumerated by the US Constitution.

This book is the author's attempt to poke fun at some of the crazier views of our current political leaders and what America might be like if Leftists were to be given unlimited political power.

Like Orwell's *1984*, this book is a warning to a new generation of the dangers of Communism and totalitarian rule.

Connect With *EM Cooter!*

Share your opinions,
learn what else is in store, and
join in the fight against Leftism in America…

Subscribe: www.subscribepage.com/emcooter

Email: em@emcooter.com

Facebook: facebook.com/IamEMCooter

Twitter: @realemcooter